VISION, COURAGE, *and* DETERMINATION

A Century of Cross-Border Social Work

Edited by Jean Ayoub and Peter van Vliet

with contributors from across the ISS network

INTERNATIONAL SOCIAL SERVICE

PEN & PUBLISH

International Social Service – General Secretariat

32, Quai du Seujet
1201 Geneva
Switzerland
+41 22 906 77 00
www.iss-ssi.org
info@iss-ssi.org

Published by Pen & Publish, LLC, USA

PEN&
PUBLISH

Saint Louis, Missouri
+1 (314) 827-6567
www.PenandPublish.com
info@PenandPublish.com

Illustrations © Hani Abbas

Editing Jean Ayoub, Peter van Vliet

Publishing Coordination Sabina Titarenko

Paperback ISBN: 978-1-956897-56-2

ebook ISBN: 978-1-956897-57-9

Cite as *Vision, Courage, and Determination. A Century of Cross-Border Social Work* (International Social Service, 2024).

Contents

Chapter 1: Vision to Change

Ambassador Susan Jacobs (Retired), Chair, Governing Board
International Social Service, Board member International Social
Service USA

Julie Rosicky, CEO, International Social Service USA

*"In a time of mass destruction and mass population movements there was some
audacity in this project with its insistence on the importance of each individual,
of his personal hopes and plans and his social ties."*[1]

As we celebrate the 100th anniversary of the founding of International
Social Service, we believe it is important to reflect upon our past and
to prepare for the future. ISS has endured and persevered for 100 years
because of its ability to envision, respond, and adapt to change. We adapt
our methodologies but always with a laser focus on our bedrock principle:
the importance of the individual.

People have been moving around the world from time immemorial
– often at great risk and danger, especially to women and children. At
the World Young Women's Christian Association (YWCA) conference
in Stockholm in 1914, motivated by growing unrest throughout Europe,
some of the delegates determined to bring an intercountry focus to this
problem. However, the vicissitudes of war prevented the World YWCA
from meeting again until 1920.

At the 1920 meeting, this group of educated women, practicing social
workers, was still working for the YWCA's Immigration Service Bureau,
National Department for Work with Foreign Born Women. They were in
their late 20s or early 30s, and single-minded about making a difference in
the world: idealistic and eager to make their ideals a reality. They were ready
to travel to far-flung places and get their boots muddy. They were articulate
advocates, witty writers, speakers, visionaries, architects, scholars, teachers,

---

1. Mary Hurlbutt, "Introduction" in Ruth Larned, "International Social Service, A
History, 1921–1955," (International Social Service, 1956).

5

surveyors, and, importantly, friends. They were bound by a common mission: to understand the impacts of migration. While the group of social workers included women from the United States of America (US), Britain, France, Greece, Switzerland, the then Czechoslovakia, and Poland, the focus in this chapter is on the women from the US as emblematic of all the women involved.

The effects of migration on women and children

"No one who knew them well could hold the comfortable theory that the hardships suffered by steerage passengers were always temporary or insignificant."[2]

As these women came to know the many foreign-born living among them, they learned about their acute needs that arose "as a result of the terrible disruption and mangling of family life during the war."[3] In particular, these migrants were worried about how they would communicate with their loved ones abroad, search for those who were lost, bring orphaned children and elderly family members to the US, and "bridge the chasm of broken communication."[4] Those travelling abroad or who needed to travel to another country were concerned about how to gain access to information about travel, completing affidavits and securing certificates of birth or marriage.

It is important to remember that means of travel were limited primarily to steamships. "Those working to assist the migrants were often quickly lost among immigration laws, steamship regulations, the difficulties of transferring money . . . and the maze of interlocking conditions that affect immigrant families."[5] The steamship companies were not interested in their passengers' individual circumstances or whether they would be admitted to their country of destination. They were simply interested in how a person would pay for their passage.

These YWCA social workers studied the consequences of denial of entry through the careful analysis of deportation cases to understand the services

2. Mary E. Hurlbutt, "The Development of International Case Work," National Department for Work with Foreign Born Women, Young Women's Christian Association, 1922.

3. Hurlbutt, "Development of International Case Work."

4. Hurlbutt, "Development of International Case Work."

5. Hurlbutt, "Development of International Case Work."

needed if the women and children returned to their countries of origin as well as what was needed to reapply for entry to the United States. They learnt that steamships had vastly different methods of handling deportees, from absolutely abominable conditions to well-accompanied transfers with assistance at the port at the other end of the journey. There were cases of children separated from their families upon arrival at Ellis Island in New York and lost for months, only to be found later in an orphanage in a transit country, having never reached their planned destination. In other cases, migrants were found "dumped across a border, penniless and with no way to reach home."[6] Migrants were often stopped at ports of entry because the spelling of a name did not match an affidavit, birth certificate, or marriage certificate. Or migrants simply did not understand what was being asked of them due to language barriers or lack of access to information. In other cases, they were unaware of new immigration laws in the US and other countries that limited the number of migrants from a particular country. They would have sold their very last belongings, arrived at the border only to be denied entry for one reason or another, and sent back home, with no one and nothing to return to.

The YWCA social workers also looked for research or information that could shed light on the impacts of migration. What they found was inaccurate or racially biased, and the only "energetic efforts" to understand and protect travellers were efforts by a number of national committees to suppress the white slave traffic.[7]

These YWCA social workers were undaunted by what they had learnt and what information was clearly missing. They travelled overseas on a variety of missions. Mary Hurlbutt spent time in the then Czechoslovakia developing and providing a social work training programme. Eight American social workers from the US and other missions in Europe, along with twenty-eight Czech social workers, lived together in an old castle on the outskirts of Prague.[8] Together they developed a basic social work training programme that tested American methodologies and created the opportunity to adapt the training to the needs of the Czech people.

---

6. Hurlbutt, "Development of International Case Work."

7. Hurlbutt, "Development of International Case Work."

8. Mary E. Hurlbutt, "Transplanting the American Brand of Social Work," *The Family* 1, no. 7 (November 1920).

Anna Kempshall, a social worker from New York, became so interested in family problems related to immigration that in 1922, she resigned from The Charity Organization Society of the City of New York (COS), where she had been working with immigrants in New York City. She joined the newly formed International Migration Service as associate director, doing the same work internationally she had done locally in New York. In order to gain firsthand knowledge of the problems facing immigrant families, she first visited Ellis Island to work with officials there and then travelled to Turkey, Greece, France, and England to gain deeper experience.[9]

Ruth Larned worked with the settlement house movement, which involved the educated and privileged residing in poor and often immigrant communities sharing their education and frequently their religious beliefs. This movement quickly transformed into an opportunity to learn about these communities and to assist them to meet their social, health, work, family, and educational needs. In working with those foreign born in the settlement houses, Ruth got to know many Greek, Armenian, Russian, and Turkish immigrants and, through these encounters, was inspired to serve overseas as well.[10] Ruth had a deep understanding of immigration law and the predicaments in which it placed families. In particular, foreign-born women with naturalised husbands and US-born children in the 1920s were not afforded US citizenship through marriage and instead had to undergo the naturalisation process separately. Ruth became a constant and fierce advocate to amend and change US laws to overcome or prevent family separation.

Through time spent working with foreign-born families in the US and with families at points of departure, these YWCA women were building the blueprints of an entirely new way of doing social work, based on their understanding of problems both at home and abroad.

---

9. John E. Hansan, "Anna (Star) Kempshall (1892–1961): Prominent social worker, long-time director of the Family Service Department of the Community Service Society of New York," Social Welfare History Project, retrieved October 2, 2024, https://socialwelfare.library.vcu.edu/eras/great-depression/kempshall-anna-star-1891-1961-social-worker-director-family-service-department-css.

10. Roxana Banu, "Forgotten Female Actors in Private International Law," in *Portraits of Women in International Law*, ed. Immi Tallgren (Oxford University Press, 2023).

The development of a new field: "International casework"

Mary Hurlbutt and others developed a terminology for the work that they were doing assisting families both in foreign countries and in the United States. *International casework* was the provisional term they chose for the variety of services rendered to individuals when those services dealt with social factors in two or more countries.[11] Hurlbutt went on to say, "... it is not so important what we call this work, whether it's international case work, or international adjustment or international information service." The authors are glad they chose "casework" over the other options.

But what Mary and others believed was of the utmost importance was using a consistent methodology and technique. It was essential that records be kept with all the necessary details so that any colleagues could pick up a correspondence or a case file and understand what was happening, what needed to happen, and what was required to resolve the case. The archival records of ISS-USA contain large file folders, often more than a couple of inches thick, tied in a ribbon that disintegrated once unfastened, containing carefully typed letters on onion skin paper, fraying at the corners, which laid out in meticulous detail examples of correspondence on cases.

Also of importance was language accessibility. Much of the correspondence was translated from English to another language such as German or French. When times were lean for ISS members, often the directors would type letters and other documents themselves in English if neither a typist nor an interpreter was affordable. Although training was sorely needed, the YWCA workers knew that there was no training specifically for this work: they were forging an entirely new discipline. The workers thought of themselves as in a perpetual state of "self-training" and in the process of being "self-trained."

It soon became clear that a permanent programme to help all migrants, not just single women, would involve specialised knowledge and the need to create a centralised office where all in the endeavour would be able to collaborate and learn from the others in developing casework skills. For example, if social workers in the US were trying to help social workers in France resolve a particular issue, capturing their methodology and what worked would be useful to help France resolve a similar future cross-border issue with the then Czechoslovakia. Pooling information, centralising

---

11. Hurlbutt, "Development of International Case Work."

methods, developing best practices, and preventing duplication were all necessary to continue with the process of "self-training" and harmonizing methodologies. Furthermore, it was essential for these women to create effective relationships with government immigration authorities and other government and nongovernment actors so that they each in turn had others to call upon if the scope of the request went beyond their knowledge base or ability to intervene.

Consideration of the needs of the individual

Finally, the women, through their vast experiences as case workers, determined that it was essential to put the needs of the individual at the centre of this "international casework," as this was not the sole purpose of other governmental or nongovernmental entities.[12]

"There is an urgent need for further development of this system in other countries and for coordination by international convention. But no international convention can supply the machinery which will meet each individual's needs. For a long time, it will be a voluntary initiative which will meet each individual's needs. For a long time, it will be a voluntary initiative which must fill in the gaps and secure the delicate and resourceful adjustment of each individual's problem."[13]

Advanced planning *before* migrating or being deported

"It may be possible in the future to work out a co-operative scheme . . . whereby receiving information regarding each case in advance, it (the receiving country) would furnish provisional care and then facilitate whatever else is needed for the long term."[14]

Social workers seeking to help migrants, as well as the migrants themselves, were often unprepared for what lay ahead. Those migrating were more, or just as, traumatised by what they encountered on their journey than if they had remained at home. International casework, therefore, demanded that actors on both sides of a border alert the necessary service providers so that people could be well prepared to travel with some assurance that they had

---

12. Hurlbutt, "Development of International Case Work."

13. Hurlbutt, "Development of International Case Work."

14. Hurlbutt, "Development of International Case Work."

what was needed to gain admittance. In addition, they also needed to have a plan as to where they were going upon reaching their destination and how they would get there. One can imagine a note safety-pinned inside a worn woollen coat containing the precious address of how to find the loved one upon arrival. Similarly, in cases of returns, or deportations, there needed to be a plan for the person to be received and provided shelter upon arrival. If there was onward travel from the port of entry, there needed to be a plan and funding to support that person to reach their final destination.

The YWCA workers were undaunted by the unimaginable hardships facing the migrants. While many would have found the migrants' predicaments insurmountable, they were, instead, inspired. Despite being separated by borders, languages, and cultures and in a perpetual state of "self-training," they persevered. As Anna Kempshall wrote, "the only absolutely basic and generalized concept (to doing this work) seems to be a sense of humour."[15]

What came next?

"It is difficult to foreshadow what sort of centralized service one ought to ultimately hope for . . . We must enlarge our understanding to fit the scope of the immigrant's experience—we must multiply resources so that we can meet his need at every point. Our problem is to conserve the accuracy, the flexibility and the sensitive personal relations most often developed by local private effort and yet to find an instrument for larger service required. . . . It is with the courage born of a sense of the neglect of this problem and its urgency during these post-war years that the YWCA has undertaken to develop an emigration service program for women in its constituent societies. The widespread and yet intimate touch of associations with the lives of women in every sort of community should give wisdom to our plans and should enable us to not only to ensure a safer journey but a wiser decision in starting and a happier adjustment in the new home."[16]

---

15. "Official proceedings of the annual meeting: 1925," in the digital collection National Conference on Social Welfare Proceedings: 677, accessed October 2, 2024, https://quod.lib.umich.edu/n/ncosw/ACH8650.1925.001/692?rgn=full+text&view=image.

16. Mary E. Hurlbutt, "In the service of the migrants," *The International Woman Suffrage News*, May 1, 1921: 15, 8 in Gernitsen Women's History Collection of Aletta H. Jacobs: iv.

The miracle of loose change: The beginning of a new organisation

At the 1920 YWCA world meeting in Champéry, Switzerland, delegates representing seventeen countries made the official decision to work together rather than continue to act independently. They agreed to survey "the nature and extent of the problems involved in migration . . . in order to stimulate coordinated action."[17] A Standing Migration Committee to gather the relevant data was appointed and directed to report back to the world conference in 1921. The report would become the "Welfare of Migrants."

The report was printed just before a meeting in Geneva on August 2, 1921, for the International Emigration Commission set up by the International Labour Office (ILO). Prior to the report's release, the YWCA Standing Committee on Migration created general principles for the experimental bureau: offices should be created at critical points of migration, the best possible records should be kept to become the basis of future study, and the service should be without discrimination as to nationality, race, religion, or political affiliation. Although willing to take responsibility for starting the work, the YWCA aimed to relinquish control as soon as an independent structure could be organised to house this newly developed network. Service bureaux were established in places where the YWCA women had already developed strong relationships: Prague, Warsaw, Paris, Cherbourg, Le Havre, Antwerp, Athens, and Constantinople (now Istanbul).[18]

Meanwhile, efforts were underway to fund this "growing experiment" as an independent structure. The religious basis of the YWCA was a hindrance to an organisation that would not discriminate based on religion. In addition, the work needed to expand beyond serving "young women" to include migrating women, children, and families and to include a specialisation in casework skills.

Fast-forward to 1924. Four young women, out of the many women involved in this initial project, became the clear expedition leaders in this new venture. The challenges they faced were formidable. Foremost, the fact that they were women at a time when women had little agency, were denied the vote in many countries, and had little direct influence

---

17. Ruth Larned, "International Social Service, A History, 1921–1955," (International Social Service, 1956).

18. Larned, "International Social Service, A History, 1921–1955."

over governmental policies. As social workers, they had to figure out how to internationalise their efforts. They met as volunteers outside of their professional jobs, calling themselves "the committee on the universe," and set about a plan to raise the necessary funds, as the wartime funding of the YWCA and other organisations had long dried up. They needed to turn the experiment into a proper organisation. At one of their late-evening sessions, they realised they had no money even to employ a secretary to type the appeal. They emptied their pocketbooks into a pile on the floor and found they could carry on for a week. One week turned into three weeks and then into many more weeks, months, and years.

It is interesting to note that to this day, no one in ISS is quite sure who all four members of the "committee on the universe" were. However, this is not critically important because this nascent organisation held a deep belief that "the strength of the ISS has always lain, and must continue to lie, not in individuals, but in their collective effort, in group wisdom and in the development of mutual understanding."[19]

The funds raised in the first week enabled the women to carry on for another three months and the opportunity to not only raise funds in the US, but also to set an example and stimulate fundraising in other partner countries. In doing so, this infant network avoided the pitfall of relying too heavily on American funds and enabled each member to build relationships, awareness, and funding support in their local communities.

Their impassioned pleas recruited steadfast and loyal board members and benefactors. Mrs. Elinor Prudden Burns was one such person, who served on the ISS-USA board from 1925 to 1967. She was an ardent supporter and raised a great deal of money to support ISS-USA's work, and she even gave anonymously to Ruth Larned's retirement fund. The women of ISS took care not only of their organisation and the individuals they served, but one another.

Financially speaking, ISS members have always been a frugal lot. At one time, the ISS-USA office used orange milk crates as filing cabinets. "The European branch directors unable to afford bilingual secretaries, typed their own letters in English. They were just too absorbed in keeping the work alive to pay much heed to impediments."[20]

---

19. Hurlbutt, "Development of International Case Work."

20. Larned, "International Social Service, A History, 1921–1955."

Why is change a good thing?

ISS members remain so committed to their mission that many still operate on "shoestring" budgets, and some have teetered on the brink of insolvency. Some members kept the work alive on an entirely voluntary basis, some had to close, and some took shelter under the auspices of larger organisations. Where ISS members have closed, different member organisations have been recruited. Over the years, the network has grown slowly to include new partners, due to the changing geopolitical landscape from migration flows, climate change, and warfare.

Similarly, over the years, funding patterns have shifted away from reliance on national government funding to favouring private grants, fundraising appeals, and funding from individuals or local entities that need services overseas. There are always some exceptions where governments still pay largely for services, or ISS is housed within a government ministry. Regardless of the source of the funding, there are several constants, initiated by our founders, that have continued throughout our first 100 years.

We learn from the past and commit to the future

The founders imagined in 1921 that "the best possible records should be kept with the intent that they can become the basis of future study."[21] And this is exactly what has come to pass. ISS-USA, ISS Greece, ISS Japan, and the General Secretariat all have collections of archives. ISS-USA's administrative files are part of the University of Minnesota Social Welfare Archives: "the most loved and used collection," according to their archivist, Linnea Anderson, of all the University's holdings. These files, covering many decades, contain the personal stories of thousands of people affected by the work of ISS-USA and whichever ISS network partner(s) they were working with overseas.

Starting in the late 1940s and into the 1950s, ISS became involved with intercountry adoption. The ISS-USA archives have provided a wealth of information for adult adoptees who have later searched for information about their origins and for living family members to potentially connect with. In addition, dozens of researchers have conducted archival research that has brought to light ISS adoption practices and ISS's concern from the

---

21. Larned, "International Social Service, A History, 1921–1955."

very beginning as to whether intercountry adoption was the best choice for every child and in what other ways ISS could support a child's connections to their family. From this research, the ISS network has advocated for a more cautionary approach to intercountry adoption. This includes ISS's involvement in helping to develop private international law to refine and regulate adoption practices to be centered on the rights and protection of the child. ISS has also advocated for ensuring adult adoptees are able to access information about their past and has developed expertise in family tracing and facilitating reunifications among family members.

Research into the cases in the ISS-USA administrative archives provides insight into the issues for which the ISS network advocates. These include private international law issues including child support, international parental child protection, intercountry adoption, and the UN Convention on the Rights of the Child. In addition, case research has informed ISS good practice guides on children on the move, surrogacy, and safe alternative care, to name a few.

Today, ISS is present in more than 120 countries, and many ISS partners work with between fifty and a hundred countries each year. ISS has persevered through wars and conflicts, climate events, political crises, and global pandemics. Despite the proliferation of global conventions and more robust consular services, the need for ISS's work is enduring. As Mary Hurlbutt said, ". . . there will always be a need for a voluntary initiative which must fill in the gaps and secure the delicate and resourceful adjustment of each individual's problem."[22] By cutting through the inevitable red tape, ISS meets the challenges in the same ways its founders did: with detailed case notes and advocacy for solutions that are in the best interest of the individual.

In conclusion, in thinking about what international casework will mean to future generations of children and families who will be migrating or separated for reasons we have yet to comprehend, there is one certainty: ISS will strive to understand these challenges and develop creative solutions to assist cross-border families with the same kind, passionate, unbiased, objective approach that has been part of our audacious DNA for the last 100 years. ISS has the vision to change.

---

22. Larned, "International Social Service, A History, 1921–1955."

Chapter 2: Curiosity to Explore

Baitzar Mardikian Gazerian, General Secretary of the Board, ISS Greece, member of the ISS Governing Board

The International Social Service (ISS) is an organisation that has survived for 100 years. This indicates its long-standing ability to deal with difficult and urgent problems under pressing situations in multicultural settings. Effective programmes necessitate learning about others, their beliefs, their needs, their aspirations, their culture, their values, their modes of life, their biases, their perceptions of the world. But prior to learning about others, it is important to learn about oneself. To explore who I am, which values and principles determine my behaviour, what are my biases, and are my actions and behaviours in accordance with my beliefs and values? Any answer should not be given in a hurry. Frequently we come across people and find a great deal of discrepancy between their words and deeds.

ISS is an organisation that has brought about change and continues to be a change agent for individuals, families, groups, and communities. Social work is a change agent, but to achieve change, education and exploration are necessary.

ISS has explored best practices by offering training programmes to prepare those who will work in the organisation. In the early years, this was often done in difficult situations and with limited resources, human and financial. Today, conditions are different – better in some cases and probably worse in others. Let us consider exploration and the capacity of ISS to explore new frameworks for effective social work across borders.

I would like to refer to social work and its role in *informal* exploration and education, which through its everyday contact and communication with individuals, families, organisations, and communities transmits to them values, skills, modes of behaviour, and so forth. Social workers have formal professional education, which contributes to their self-knowledge, and the acquisition of theoretical knowledge and skills applicable in accordance with what needs to be dealt with. Due to political and economic developments, communities undergo changes, directly influencing almost everyone. We have refugees and we have immigrants (legal or not), all in the quest for a better life in countries considered "safe" and "prosperous." But the so-called "safe" and "influential" countries feel the need to raise fences to protect themselves and their culture from "invaders," while at the same time, they are not locally protected from juvenile delinquency, criminality, fraud, poverty, and so on. Social work has to offer services both to those who are in the protected, "fenced" area, but also to those who trespass within it, to offer *education* to overcome the difficulties and problems that create undesirable behaviour and also to *educate* the newcomers to learn about the new culture and its demands.

ISS holds values like those found in social work. Social workers, in general, as well as those working for ISS, have an important role in transmitting these values to individuals, families, groups, and communities. It may be utopian to believe that this will make the world better, but it definitely improves the situation of some people. Let us consider this using information that comes from the International Federation of Social Workers (IFSW).

The global definition of the social work profession states, "social work is a practice-based profession and an academic discipline that promotes social change and development, social cohesion, and the empowerment and liberation of people. Principles of social justice, human rights, collective responsibility, and respect for diversity are central to social work. Underpinned by theories of social work, social sciences, humanities and indigenous knowledge, social work engages people and structures in order to address life challenges and enhance wellbeing." This definition was approved by the IFSW General Meeting and the IASSW[23] General Assembly in July 2014.

The core mandates of the above definition include promoting social change, development, and cohesion, accompanied by the empowerment and liberation of people. My purpose is not to analyse mandates and principles but to use some examples to show how informal education and exploration take place. A basic element in social work is the direct communication between social worker and client, and the establishment of a relationship. Over the last few years, the use of different technologies – the telephone, email, internet – is increasingly being used alone or as complementary methods in the delivery of therapeutic services. Extended research is necessary before their widespread adoption. In the delivery of theoretical knowledge, they may be quite adequate, but in the development

---

23. IASSW is the International Association of Schools of Social Work.

of communication and the establishment of a relationship in order to deal with problems of interpersonal relations, the use of the internet is questionable. The acquisition of theoretical knowledge is one thing; the development of relationship-building skills is another.

Social work is not a bureaucratic profession. It is a job that, through the relationship developed between the social worker and the client, enables the individual to develop self-confidence, improve their self-image, learn to trust others, and cooperate to achieve their goals. The social worker does not impose himself or his suggestions in order to solve problems.

When I was a student, the first thing we learnt was "start where the client is." While a lot of things have changed since then, the relation of the social worker with the individual (regardless of whether we term him a client or something else) is a unique relationship and becomes the means of change. The process from the beginning to the achievement of the goals set by the client and the worker is a helping process as well as a learning process. The person learns to assess his situation, find the causes that create the problem(s), develop goals, plan for the needed activities, and find the necessary resources in himself and the environment. Through the process, the individual experiences respect, dignity, and worth as a person. He learns how to handle his anger in cases of social injustice and, at the same time, can make his needs known, defend his ideas, support his views, and overcome his fears.

The work of the social worker is not limited to the individual. The work with families and groups helps individuals to deal with interpersonal relations, learn to listen, become responsible, be responsive to the needs of others, and work together for the achievement of a common goal. The individual learns how to use power and how to deal with oppression, be able to set limits but also accept limits, acquire new communication skills, learn methods of dealing with conflict, understand processes of decision-making, and plan for goal achievement. They have the opportunity in the safe environment of the group to test these newly acquired skills.

Another important area of intervention is the community. Of course, prior to any intervention, a thorough knowledge of what is occurring in the community is critical. Often there are conflicting interests, a reluctance or a resistance to change, a lack of acceptance, the rejection of newcomers or new ideas, and scapegoating. The social worker can become a coordinator who can work with conflicting groups to settle differences, identify the causes of conflicts, provide means for understanding, and teach techniques in an informal way.

The social worker, because of his or her training, has learnt to deal with conflict with patience, in a disciplined manner, not allowing emotions to influence thinking and judgment, not taking sides, and able to arbitrate and also advocate. These skills are practiced by the social worker and, at the same time, those participating in the different groups who have the experience of dealing with known problems in new ways. The process of change may be long, at times disappointing, but the results are long-lasting. The participants experience new situations, learn new skills applicable in other groups, and then teach others; all this happens in a democratic manner. Last but not least, they have the opportunity to participate in developing and applying programmes to meet their needs.

Social workers are change agents not only of people, but also of systems. This creates a situation that may be considered ambiguous. Can one be in a system applying its guidelines and on the other try to change it when it is dysfunctional? This is neither a problem nor a contradiction. The social worker is a person, a citizen, and therefore, as a professional (social worker) functions as an employee, but as a citizen, they can join groups that strive to change situations in the interests of the people in accordance with the values of social work. Human needs change, but the change of systems is slow and undesirable for some. One should not forget the power games played in societies, which may contradict or undermine held values.

The international and national declarations of human rights, women and children's rights, the rights of people with disabilities, refugee rights, and the conventions and meetings at high levels that take place to decide on the well-being of all people are well known. However, those of us working in the field as informed citizens know the extent to which they are applied, not to mention some double standards. Many of the people served by the different organisations unfortunately have negative experiences. How does an oppressed individual feel in an autocratic system? How do people feel when their daily life is war and fear? Or the child who in an effort to find a "better" life loses his family? Or the adults who due to successive crises have lost the means to deal with their own or their family's daily needs? How does the woman left alone with her children feel? How do all those who find themselves in foreign countries experience their lives not knowing the language or about existing services or the different culture? I can give many more examples, but this is unnecessary. Similar conditions were the impetus for the foundation of ISS.

Ruth Larned, in "International Social Service, A History 1921–1955" describes very vividly the conditions that necessitated the creation of ISS, and it is not a surprise that among the founders were social workers. ISS was founded after the First World War, with financial and economic crises, and then the Second World War, and the continuing effects from many wars (including in Korea, Vietnam, African countries including genocides, Ukraine-Russia, and Palestine-Israel). Also, there are the negative effects of climate change and other negative results of human activities on nature. All these conditions and events have their impact on countries and people. Old and new problems need old and new ways of dealing with them. The experience of the past should help, technology also may play its part, but the core help will come from devoted people willing to work towards a more just and integrated society. Let us hope that the years ahead will be more peaceful and that the values of ISS, through its work, will be transmitted to ever larger groups of people. ISS will continue to explore for a better world through international collaboration and best practice social work across borders.

Chapter 3: Courage to Dare

Apolline Foedit, PhD candidate, Research Assistant, the Geneva Graduate Institute

The International Social Service (ISS) stands as a centennial organisation; its history intertwines with the broader history of human rights. In this chapter, we unpack its role in codifying children's rights, thanks to its archives. These documents encompass a diverse array of materials, ranging from concise casework reports to correspondence, commentary on draft documents and conventions, presentations, and brochures. My choice of title, "Courage to Dare," encapsulates the ethos of ISS members: they exhibit audacity in taking action, confronting challenges head-on, and innovating novel solutions, all driven by their dedication to the well-being of children and families.

Organised into three sections, this chapter delves into pivotal moments in the advancement of children's rights, with a focus on ISS's contributions during key junctures in 1924, 1959, and 1989. These dates, steeped in significance, mark the signing of three seminal documents. Yet, beyond their legal significance, lies a narrative rich in complexity – a narrative of fervent advocacy, of networks interwoven, and of individuals shaping the destiny of children's rights. Indeed, it was amid the late nineteenth and early twentieth centuries that specialised reform networks blossomed, nurturing the seeds of child protection.[24]

But where did ISS find its place amid these burgeoning networks of change makers? How did it navigate the corridors of power within the newly formed League of Nations and later within the United Nations?

Within this web of advocacy, ISS members found themselves entwined with other esteemed figures, forging alliances within the chambers of the International Committee of the Red Cross (ICRC) and the International

---

24. Joëlle Droux, "L'internationalisation de la protection de l'enfance: acteurs, concurrences et projets transnationaux (1900–1925)," Critique internationale 52, no. 3 (2011) [Translation: "The Internationalisation of Child Protection: Actors, Competition, and Transnational Projects (1900–1925)," International Critics 52, no. 3 (2011)]: 17–33.

Union for Child Welfare (IUCW). One notable figure among them is Suzanne Ferrière, who emerged as a guiding force from the organisation's inception. Her trajectory, from the trenches of the Civilian Service of the Central Agency for Prisoners of War under the mentorship of her uncle, Frédéric Ferrière, to the helm of ISS, speaks about the organisation's resilience. Moreover, Suzanne's close collaboration with Eglantyne Jebb was instrumental in the establishment of the Save the Children International Union and, later, the International Union for Child Welfare (IUCW).

Embark with us on this journey through time, resilience, and the pursuit of justice, all illuminated by the work of the International Social Service.

First steps in internationalizing children's rights: The 1924 Declaration of the Rights of the Child as a pioneering milestone in children's rights history

The genesis of the 1924 League of Nations' Declaration of the Rights of the Child is a narrative intertwined with the threads of social reforms, humanitarian endeavours, and the collaborative spirit among emerging international institutions and transnational movements dedicated to advancing children's rights.

Since the end of the nineteenth century, reform movements had been addressing the dire circumstances endured by children across various spheres, from labour and antitrafficking to justice and education, and advocating for social and legal measures to better their plight. Central to this effort was the establishment of the Association Internationale pour la Protection de l'Enfance (AIPE) in Brussels in 1913, serving as a hub for information gathering and technical expertise provision to governments and private entities alike.

World War I and its aftermath exacerbated the plight of children across Europe, leaving them displaced, sick, and starving. Among the myriad organisations rising to meet this need was the Save the Children Fund (SCF), founded by British reformers Dorothy Buxton and Eglantyne Jebb. Collaborating with the International Committee of the Red Cross, the SCF played a pivotal role in the creation of the Geneva-based Save the Children International Union (SCIU) in 1920. Amid these efforts, the groundwork for ISS was being laid, with its eventual members already deeply involved in this humanitarian ecosystem. By 1920, the urgent necessity for a Standing Migration Committee to address international migration issues was acknowledged, leading to the establishment of the International Migration Service (later renamed ISS). It initially operated as a department of the World Young Women's Christian Association based in London.

The inception of the League of Nations in 1919, heralding the dawn of the first intergovernmental organisation tasked with fostering global peace and cooperation, provided a platform for various institutions dedicated to international child protection, including the AIPE and the SCIU, to converge and sometimes compete.

In 1924, the Committee for the Protection of Children was established within the League of Nations, serving as a consultative body engaging both governmental bodies and private organisations. Notably, this committee played a crucial role in collecting information and facilitating the evolution of national legislation concerning children's rights. It was also instrumental in adopting the Declaration of the Rights of the Child in 1924, a document originally formulated by the SCIU the previous year.

This Declaration articulated the fundamental needs of children in five key points, acknowledging their inherent rights to both material and spiritual development, assistance, relief in times of distress, protection from exploitation in the workplace, and support to nurture their talents for the greater good. The establishment of the Committee for the Protection of Children and the subsequent adoption of the Geneva Declaration marked pivotal moments not only in the history of childhood, but also in the realm of international relations.

In 1924, a significant milestone occurred for ISS as it gained independence, marking the beginning of its history. Tasked with facilitating casework spanning multiple countries and dedicated to the noble cause of reuniting families separated by vast distances, ISS pioneered innovative approaches that took into consideration the complex interplay of social, legal, and psychological factors affecting migrants and children. Unlike many counterparts, ISS actively encouraged its members to blend legal and social work methodologies, fostering a holistic approach to addressing the needs of those they served and influencing international law. Notably, under the leadership of Ferrière, ISS advocated for the establishment of an international socio-legal framework to ensure the maintenance of families across borders, striving to rectify systemic injustices.[25] This dedication was underscored in 1925 when ISS presented a seminal report on the social challenges faced by migrating children at the inaugural Congress of Child Welfare, showcasing its commitment to tackling pressing humanitarian issues.

Other reports emerged addressing the plight of migrating children, which became even more dire during and after World War II. A primary focus was on children without families and their adoption processes.[26] ISS played a pivotal role in advancing the integration of unaccompanied minors following the Hungarian uprising in 1956, contributing to advancements in children's rights leading up to significant conventions. Notably, ISS's influence extended to the Hague Convention concerning the recognition and enforcement of decisions regarding child maintenance obligations in 1958 and the 1959 Convention on the Rights of the Child.

Continuing the journey: Exploring the 1959 Declaration of the Rights of the Child

The 1959 Declaration of the Rights of the Child was born out of the post–World War II era. It emerged from concerted efforts to reshape international discourse concerning children's rights, well-being, and protection. In 1945, two years after the creation of the United Nations Relief and Rehabilitation Administration (UNRRA) by forty-four heads of state as a transitional administrative body, the United Nations was formally established during the San Francisco Conference. The UN aimed to promote international cooperation, peace, and security among nations. This included the creation of various specialised agencies within the UN system to address issues such as health, education, and human rights.

In 1946, discussions began to have the United Nations adopt the 1924 Geneva Declaration of the Rights of the Child, leading to the creation of the United Nations International Children's Emergency Fund, known today as UNICEF. By 1950, a draft was prepared, but its presentation to

---

25. Roxana Banu, "Forgotten Female Actors in Private International Law," in Portraits of Women in International Law, ed. Immi Tallgren (Oxford University Press, 2023).

26. Heide Fehrenbach, "Children as Casework: The Problem of Migrating and Refugee Children in the Era of World War," in Research Handbook on Child Migration, eds. Jacqueline Bhabha, Daniel Senovilla Hernandez, and Jyothi Kanics (Edward Elgar, 2018).

the Assembly was delayed until 1957. Debate ensued over the necessity of a separate Declaration of the Rights of the Child alongside the Declaration of Human Rights. Eventually, on November 20, 1959, the United Nations General Assembly adopted the Declaration of the Rights of the Child, drawing from the structure and contents of the 1924 Declaration. It set out ten principles of fundamental rights for "a happy childhood," recognising that the child "by reason of his physical and mental immaturity, needs special safeguards and care, including appropriate legal protection, before as well as after birth." The endorsement of the Declaration of the Rights of the Child by the Third Commission of the UN Assembly marked a significant milestone in international child welfare efforts. Since then, every year on November 20, the United Nations celebrates International Children's Rights Day.

ISS remained unwavering in its dedication to advocating for the rights and well-being of children. Utilizing its extensive global network and deep expertise in family reunification and child welfare, ISS offered insights and support during the discussions leading to the adoption of the 1959 Declaration. Various reports, notably the one on Intercountry Adoption (1957), illuminated the challenges inherent in these discussions, underscoring the need for nuanced approaches. At the forefront of its advocacy, ISS championed the principle that the welfare of the child should be the paramount consideration in any adoption.

While the 1959 Convention was primarily declaratory in nature, it laid the groundwork for what would evolve into the United Nations Convention on the Rights of the Child (CRC), also known as the New York Convention in 1989. This foundational document already encapsulated key principles, endorsed and promoted by ISS, including the principles of equality and nondiscrimination for all children, as well as the imperative to consistently prioritise the best interests of the child.

In the ensuing years, ISS remained committed to its work for children. It continuously advocated for better laws protecting children, influencing through its practice laws regarding the maintenance obligations towards children, laws on intercountry adoption, and laws on international child abduction by parents. ISS notably provided expert knowledge and casework material to the Permanent Bureau of the Hague Conference and to the UN.

Securing children's rights: The 1989 declaration and its binding provisions

As we have seen in the two previous sections, the evolution of children's rights has been marked by significant milestones, each reflecting a collective commitment to uphold the dignity and freedom of individuals worldwide. Building upon earlier declarations, the adoption of the United Nations Convention on the Rights of the Child (CRC) in 1989 represented a turning point in the protection of children. Contrasting with the 1924 and 1959 Declarations, the 1989 CRC addressed the specific needs and rights of children in a comprehensive and legally binding manner.

The 1924 Declaration set forth foundational principles affirming the rights of children, emphasizing their entitlement to special care and protection. However, it lacked the binding legal mechanisms necessary for enforcement, rendering its impact largely declarative. Similarly, the 1959 Declaration expanded upon the rights outlined in 1924, emphasizing the importance of education, healthcare, and opportunities for children to develop to their fullest potential. Yet, like its predecessor, it lacked the enforceability required to hold nations accountable for violations of children's rights.

In contrast, the 1989 CRC represented a paradigm shift in the protection of children's rights by establishing a comprehensive framework with legally binding provisions. Unlike the earlier declarations, the CRC defines a child as any individual under the age of eighteen and articulates a wide range of civil, political, economic, social, health, and cultural rights tailored to address the specific vulnerabilities and needs of children. The 1989 CRC is also much longer than its predecessors; it is composed of fifty-four articles. From protection against exploitation to access to education and healthcare, the CRC outlines fundamental rights that every child is entitled to, regardless of nationality, ethnicity, or socioeconomic background.

According to article 3, "In all actions concerning children, whether undertaken by public or private social welfare institutions, courts of law, administrative authorities or legislative bodies, the best interests of the child shall be a primary consideration." This principle closely aligns with the core values of ISS, as we have seen, which are instrumental in navigating legal conflicts regarding children's rights, such as the delicate balance between protection and privacy or conflicts with third-party rights, including parental authority. Emphasizing the fundamental importance of the child's well-being, this principal advocates for an approach that prioritises their best interests. It encourages a participative decision-making process that recognises the foundational significance of the child's welfare.

Furthermore, the CRC established mechanisms for monitoring and enforcing its provisions, including the creation of the UN Committee on the Rights of the Child. This committee is responsible for overseeing the implementation of the convention by member states, ensuring compliance with international law and standards. States that ratified the convention are obligated to submit periodic reports and respond to inquiries regarding the status of child rights within their jurisdictions. Additionally, the CRC introduced optional protocols aimed at addressing specific issues such as child soldiers and the sale of children, further enhancing its efficacy and relevance in addressing contemporary challenges.

ISS was among the organisations that actively participated in drafting and providing feedback on the articles. Notably, ISS emphasised the significance of enshrining the right of individuals, including children, to leave any state, including their own, and to facilitate family reunification with parents or children who have left a particular country. ISS strongly advocated for the importance and centrality of the family unit in these discussions.

Celebrating progress, acknowledging challenges: The enduring legacy of the International Social Service in the journey of children's rights

In tracing the trajectory of children's rights, one cannot overlook the role played by ISS. Through its dedication, tireless advocacy, and innovative practices, ISS has left an indelible mark on the landscape of international child welfare. From its inception amid the aftermath of World War I to its instrumental contributions to the drafting and adoption of key international conventions, ISS has been a beacon of hope for countless children and families around the world.

As we reflect on the journey of children's rights, it becomes evident that the evolution of international frameworks, such as the 1924 Declaration of the Rights of the Child and the subsequent United Nations Convention on the Rights of the Child (CRC) in 1989, has been profoundly influenced by the pioneering efforts of organisations like ISS. The transition from declaratory statements to legally binding provisions underscores the progress made in safeguarding the rights and well-being of children on a global scale.

The ratification of the CRC by 196 countries by January 2024 stands as a testament to the widespread recognition of children's rights as fundamental human rights. Its enforceable provisions and comprehensive approach signify a significant milestone in the ongoing quest for justice, equality, and dignity for all individuals, especially the most vulnerable members of society.

However, despite these advancements, challenges persist, and the work of organisations like ISS remains as vital as ever. As we look towards the future, it is imperative to heed the call for continued vigilance and action in upholding the rights of the child. While progress has been made, violations still occur, reminding us that the journey towards achieving truly exemplary standards in children's rights is far from over.

Chapter 4: Desire to Cooperate

Sandrine Pepit, Director of ISS France (Foundation Droit d'Enfance)

It is difficult to begin this chapter on the desire to cooperate without mentioning the origins and founding principles of the International Social Service (ISS). Indeed, from the creation of the International Migration Service (now ISS) and before that the Young Women's Christian Association (YMCA), the question of the will and need to develop a system of cooperation quickly emerged.

In order to respond to the major migratory movements that the world experienced from the end of the nineteenth century, it was necessary to innovate and change by thinking of a collaborative model both nationally and internationally. This cooperation was fundamental to better identify and understand the needs of people in migratory situations and to develop flexible and responsive services for them in as many countries as possible.

Thanks to the conviction, dedication, and perseverance of four visionary women who surrounded themselves with professionals committed to this cause, a neutral, nondenominational, and internationally oriented organisation was born. The founders of the International Migration Service (now ISS) conceived the service in the light of the existing migration context and, above all, with the firm intention of creating links of cooperation between countries through a unique network.

Since then, the international context has continued to evolve but the fundamental issues remain similar. Nevertheless, it has been necessary to adapt the organisation's operations and areas of intervention by taking into account strong cultural specificities, immigration restrictions, and the structural change that is taking place within society.

This desire to cooperate and to help the most vulnerable people is a part of ISS's DNA. Cooperation is a founding principle and value that has resonated throughout the world over the decades. This dynamic, which was built in a complex heterogeneous environment, demonstrated, particularly at pivotal moments in history, the ability of ISS to adapt quickly to the evolution of needs and complex cross-border migration situations by taking a human and social perspective.

Even if the rationale for this cooperation between actors seems obvious, its implementation has not always been, and much remains to be done after 100 years of existence. The added value of collaborative work must be constantly reaffirmed.

The development of a unique international network with international casework expertise and regular communication between the General Secretariat and the network

To effectively launch a system of cooperation, an international network of members and partners sharing the same values and the same desire to cooperate was created in 1924. With only a few branches located mainly in Europe and America at the beginning, 100 years later, ISS has been able to consolidate its cooperation in the four corners of the world in over 120 countries. Even if the contexts and practices of social work are very different in each state, the motivation and commitment of salaried or volunteer professionals have made it possible to work with an intercultural approach and draw on other social models and practices. Indeed, the daily work of ISS requires many international interactions while respecting and preserving everyone's cultural norms and practices.

In order to put to work, mobilise, and federate its branches around the desire to work together, ISS has promoted a partnership dimension and strong cohesion by developing international casework practice sharing and standards. This casework is based on common methodologies and facilitates the sharing of experience and the enhancement of each other's expertise.

This international casework is the main activity of the branches of the ISS network and informs the leadership and policy role of the General Secretariat. The constantly evolving practices need to be revisited regularly to maintain quality casework standards and to streamline cooperation within the network.

Initially, and until a few years after the end of the Second World War, the work of ISS was mainly related to the protection and status of people in migration situations and refugees. Numerous evaluations have been carried out by all the branches around the world; this meticulous work has made it possible to be in a continuous and necessary process of collaboration.

The interdisciplinary perspective that professionals take on each situation is essential to analyse cases and then develop appropriate solutions. It also reinforces the feeling of giving meaning to their missions at the service of the people they support. This work also makes it possible to demonstrate through practice the added value of the international social work approach in a world that is constantly becoming more controlled by legalities.

To convince and ensure continuity in the management of transitional cases despite cultural differences and very disparate professional practices in social work, internal training has been designed and offered to all professionals in the network. The training courses are provided by members of the network or professionals of the General Secretariat, which allows the branches to get to know each other better and to practice better collaboration. Some training courses have also been opened externally in order to raise awareness and train professionals who were not part of the existing branches.

Over the decades, and despite the recurring difficulty of stabilising funding for all branches and the General Secretariat, members have seen the positive impact of their work on people in migration situations. To compensate for this financial instability, ISS has always been able to count on the commitment, adaptability, and innovation of its professionals, such as the implementation of reciprocity of services between branches of the network.

Finally, finding and recruiting new members and professionals are important to maintain effective collaboration and being able to adapt to changing global contexts. Thus, in order to support the formation of new connections and unique expertise, new members must be well established and have a certain reputation at the national level.

In addition, each organisation who joins the ISS network or becomes a partner must support the values and principles of ISS and, of course, add value to the network. Finding new members has always been complex, but as with each of its missions, ISS has been able to remain effective by relying on other organisations and partners to ensure the successful management of international casework. In the end, ISS has always been able to continue to serve the interests of people by relying on countless staff to carry out the casework professionally.

The need to cooperate with all the actors involved by advocating for a social work and intercultural approach

Over the past 100 years, ISS has had to adapt to constantly changing cross-border issues due to geopolitical issues with direct impacts, particularly on the evolution of migratory flows and the emergence of new forms of conflict in the private and family sphere. As a result, ISS has been regularly called upon and has always played a key role as a recognised nonpolitical, nondenominational organisation specialising in the management of complex cross-border issues.

The need for cooperation was therefore not limited to the members of the network, but also the need to involve other actors from all areas and to strike the right balance between international cooperation and national laws and regulations. ISS has always been active in national and international meetings and has campaigned extensively for recognition of the value and importance of the social dimension in the management of migration situations. ISS was also the initiator of a practice that associates private actors with international cooperation and which, in the medium and long term, has made it possible to influence public opinion, governments, and international organisations, which is still the case today.

To affirm this desire to cooperate across borders and with as many people as possible, ISS began to collaborate with various United Nations agencies at the end of the First World War, including the International Refugee Organization. In addition, one of the important milestones was the relocation of the General Secretariat to Geneva in 1925.

ISS has always wanted to bring a different and complementary perspective to the other actors concerned with the issues of migration with a focus on complex family conflicts and child protection. To this end, it has always made available all of its work and reflections related to its areas of expertise as soon as it could have an impact on the evolution of the situation of people encountering socio-legal difficulties that went beyond the borders of a single country.

ISS's research activities and the use of its analyses have enabled ISS to be identified as a privileged interlocutor by many national and international organisations and to legitimise its social intervention with people in migrant situations, especially on the international scene.

For example, one of the first studies dates back to 1926 and was entrusted to the American branch. One of its aims was to determine the legal and social consequences of immigration laws on the lives of families in conjunction with the various authorities concerned. This collaborative work has led to improved legislation and cooperation between immigration and social services.

Numerous studies and research carried out by the ISS network branches and also by the ISS General Secretariat have resulted in important socio-legal support and promoted cooperation between actors.

In addition, its mastery of a unique international casework model and its know-how in social work across borders are differentiating elements that, well established within the ISS network, have been shared and made available to international authorities and organisations. In addition, the ISS training programme has been able to be deployed and adapted to distinct audiences on an international scale since the creation of the ISS.

ISS is recognised as an expert by many international and intergovernmental organisations and also by civil society. ISS has actively contributed to numerous works that have led to the elaboration of several major international instruments related mainly to the protection of individuals, families, and minors (United Nations, Hague Conference on Private International Law).

Focus and examples of cooperation during the Second World War

The chaos and horrors of the Second World War highlighted the need for a neutral body, testifying to the solidity of the international network of ISS and its strong desire to cooperate in complex and even dangerous conditions to allow many families to be reunited. Indeed, during this period, communication between the various professionals was maintained in the majority of countries, and some, if not many, cases were managed, even with the significant challenges of that time. It should be remembered that some branches had to be closed or liquidated in several countries, including Czechoslovakia, Poland, and Greece, while others had to adapt within tight deadlines and innovate or have the obligation to develop new missions to ensure their maintenance, particularly in the United States and France.

The history of the ISS French branch, the Service Social d'Aide aux Emigrants (SSAE), shows the heroic efforts made to maintain the service. When the Germans arrived in Paris, they took over the SSAE office. Its professionals, unfortunately, had no time to destroy the archives. One of the service's professionals was able to evade the guards and entered her office in order to transfer the incriminating personal files of people of the Jewish faith to another category called "light files," which were filed under numbers and not under names. Later, she returned and convinced the occupying forces that the work of SSAE was apolitical, and so it was allowed to resume some type of service, sometimes working alongside the German Red Cross.

To finance their work, the president of the section smuggled money into Paris in her knitting yarn. Towards the end of the war, the French branch operated from Lyon and organised the emigration of Jewish children to Switzerland. The future branch leader was captured, imprisoned, and tortured and was not released until the end of the war. After the war, the French branch played a major role in providing aid and relief to nationals of countries whose agencies were no longer present in France. It also contributed to the repatriation of French nationals from abroad, including 1,200 French children cared for in Switzerland, and to the reunification of more than 900 Polish children who had been left in Poland when their parents went to work in France.

At the end of the war, four branches were still active: France, Italy, Switzerland, and the United States. The branches in Germany (1950) and Greece (1953) were reopened. But the branch in Czechoslovakia could not reopen and the one in Poland had to close. The relationships between the branches have been crucial in facilitating the movement of a significant number of people.

In 2024

Fatoumata was fourteen years old when she was forcibly married to a man in his fifties in Benin, her home country. Fatoumata unfortunately suffered terrible physical and sexual abuse. She decided to inform her parents who lived in France, who were devastated to learn of the dramatic situation in which their daughter found herself. So, they decided to try to find a way to bring her to France with them.

Fatoumata embarked on a migration journey that first led her to Turkey where, by a judge's decision, she was recognised as an unaccompanied minor and placed in a shelter to ensure her protection. The Turkish national child protection authorities, in charge of Fatoumata's case, confirmed the presence of her parents in France. They decided to contact the ISS branch in Turkey to explore the possibility of reuniting Fatoumata with her parents.

ISS Turkey thus contacted the French branch of ISS, the Fondation Droit d'Enfance, to organise an assessment at the parents' home. Subsequently, ISS France contacted the local authority responsible for collecting and assessing all information of concern relating to a minor at risk or at risk of being at risk. In this situation, after carrying out the assessment at home and collecting all the necessary information, the local authority issued an opinion in favour of the return of Fatoumata to her parents in France, with the possibility of appropriate care for the girl and support for parenthood.

ISS France then contacted the United Nations High Commissioner for Refugees (UNHCR), which, after analysing the information provided, gave a positive recommendation for family reunification.

ISS France then contacted the following:

- The local association that supports the parents and has advised them on the procedures to be followed to obtain family reunification;
- The French Ministry of Europe and Foreign Affairs to explain Fatoumata's situation and ensure follow-up for obtaining the visa; and
- Local social services to ensure that they would be able to follow Fatoumata as soon as she arrived in France.

Once the family reunification agreement was officially approved, ISS France informed ISS Turkey in order to organise and support Fatoumata's journey from Turkey to France, where she was able to reunite with her family.

In Conclusion

"In spite of difficulties of all kinds, an ever-increasing number of people all over the world, despite differences in language, laws and customs, [ISS] dedicate themselves in a daily common work, across borders, to solving the individual

problems of migrants." —Colette Laroque, member of the SSAE Honorary Board

The approach of Mary Richmont, an American social worker, according to which "the person assisted by the social worker is often called upon to rely on his or her resources and networks," is also the principle of action of ISS. Without resources or interconnections between the branches and the various actors involved, ISS would not have the same influence and expertise that is has today.

In short, the foundations of ISS are solid today thanks to visionary and pioneering women who created ISS but also thanks to all the professionals who have taken up the "torch" and continue the work initiated 100 years ago.

The professionals of the network throughout the last 100 years are all driven by the same desire to move forward together in order to help separated families across borders, in complementarity with international standards. Their commitments and efforts to promote and spread the values of mutual aid, solidarity, and sharing have made it possible to promote social work practices and to create a unique and critically important international network.[27]

---

27. This chapter is inspired by the many existing writings, but particularly by those of Ruth Larned, associate General Director of the International Social Service from 1924 to 1929, and Colette Laroque, member of the SSAE Honorary Board, SSAE Secretary General from 1964 to 1982, SSAE Administrator from 1982 to 1985.

Chapter 5: Determination to Protect

Part 1 by Lourença Lopes Moreno Tavares, President, ISS Cape Verde (ACRIDES)

The determination to protect led the International Social Service (ISS) to Cape Verde in 2013, so that, by partnering with the NGO ACRIDES, family reunification could be carried out in the best possible way. Cape Verde is a country of emigration where the people may leave their families and go in search of a better life, with Europe often the preferred destination. Amidst this mass migration, ISS – with its determination to protect – manages to reunite families and promote integration, allowing for the happiness and safety that every child and family deserve.

ISS has also contributed to the emergence of the partnership between the NGO ACRIDES and the NGO ECPAT Luxembourg. The protection of children against sexual abuse and exploitation is a great challenge and drives our determination to protect. With this partnership of seven years, ACRIDES and ECPAT Luxembourg have made a difference in the lives of many child victims of sexual abuse and exploitation and worked with the government to change laws. More organisations are now wishing to partner with ACRIDES.

Families are one of ISS's biggest challenges, and the determination to protect means that ISS members in the United States, Canada, Portugal, Guinea-Bissau, and Cape Verde can interact for the protection and defence of the rights of children and their families.

The determination to protect includes the strong will to act and requires perseverance on our part so that the results are effective and last a lifetime. The determination to protect requires much patience on our part; it requires that we have the skills required to perform effective intercountry casework. In the determination to protect, it is not enough to say that I am a leader – we must lead with great love and dedication for all of humanity.

The determination to protect requires that we commit fully to those who need protection to make them safe so they can fall and get back up and continue their journey of inclusion. We serve those in need of warmth, love, and emotional stability. We serve those who are weakened by the struggle of life, and we help them regain control in their lives. We must always act in the best interest of all humanity.

The determination to protect requires us to confront the worst in the world and take on people who seek to do harm by violence, oppression, war, or discrimination. We support the most vulnerable, including children, families, and older people impacted by cross-border separation. We work towards a better world for all with over 100 years of innovation to support every child and family to get the best of what life offers them.

Part 2 by Sylvie J. Lapointe, MSW, Executive Director, ISS Canada

"This is the story of how, out of dawning awareness of the unnecessary waste and tragedy in the lives of transplanted people, there grew a determination to discover the means by which migration might become a less destructive experience, and, if possible, one of real value."[28]

And so, it began: the determination to protect. By wanting to explore and find ways to make migration less destructive, the founders of ISS set an ideal service in place that would help humankind. A service that would be better for all involved in difficult situations. In 100 years, many things have changed, but much remains the same. Humans are on the move, facing difficult life-changing events, and there are agencies that help and protect, such as ISS, which throughout its existence has protected people across borders.

In everything that ISS undertakes, writes, produces, and puts into action, there is the common thread: protection. Most of the ISS members work with children and families that are facing difficult situations. Whether by working with children in the child protection system, unaccompanied minors, or families seeking refuge from difficult situations in their country of origin, ISS is asked to play a role that will have the impact to protect – a role that will permit one to feel safe, to feel understood, to feel secure, and to feel able to leave some of their troubles behind and no longer need that protection – and that is liberating.

---

28. Larned, "International Social Service, A History, 1921–1955."

Thousands of case examples are available from the ISS network. How by using the expertise of ISS, the outcome of the case was one of making a difficult situation, a dangerous situation, feel bearable.

Let us look at this case example from Germany: A British mother, who had a history of mental illness and received ongoing care from the British Social Service, travelled around Europe with her three-year-old daughter for months without any money. In the summer of 2000, she had already attracted attention in Italy, and the local authorities had concerns about the daughter's adequate care. The Italian branch of ISS was able to obtain background information from England. Before they could offer services, the mother had already left Italy. She had indicated that she wanted to travel to Austria or Germany. The ISS British branch office informed ISS in Germany and in Austria about the family in case the mother and daughter were located. A few months later, the British embassy shared the information that the mother had spent the night in a homeless shelter in Berlin. Again, before any help could be provided, the mother and daughter disappeared again. A few days later, her mother went to the hospital for treatment, and her daughter went to the local child protection in Berlin. The child protection agency contacted the father who was still in England, was very worried about the girl, and immediately expressed his willingness to come to Berlin to pick her up. However, the father did not have custody of the daughter. With the help of both ISS Germany and ISS UK (and in following the right legal steps), and with much mediation, wanting to protect the best interest of the child throughout this ordeal, the child was, in the end, sent to live with her father. Services were also put in place to make sure the mother received the help she required and that her rights as a mother (to continue her relationship with her daughter) were protected.

This is a great example of an everyday case where protection is what drives ISS and its dedicated professionals. But ISS is more than just casework. Protection also happens at other levels of ISS.

The International Reference Centre (IRC)

The International Reference Centre (IRC) for children deprived of their family is part of the ISS network. Over thirty years ago, the ISS General Secretariat founded the IRC. The IRC promotes the exchange of knowledge, experience, and dialogue between professionals of governmental and nongovernmental agencies throughout the world. The IRC's principal goal is to provide alternative care and adoption professionals with professional information to assist in their daily work by developing resources and highlighting best practices and, in doing so, promoting the protection of children. Likewise, the IRC aims to raise awareness of the need to protect children's rights within the analytical framework of international standards in an ever-changing environment. Today, more than 5,000 professionals in countries of origin and receiving countries directly benefit from IRC services. The IRC is a wealth of knowledge of resources on everything about children and child protection in its broad sense and protection in all situations (including adoption and foster care). The ISS network can rely on the IRC to provide expertise and advice when developing policy, writing advocacy position papers, and providing advice in complicated cases.

ISS projects and advocacy papers

Let's start with the project that has been implemented in numerous countries: A Better Future is Possible. Started in 2014 by the General Secretariat, with the expertise of professionals, the project aims to find safe, permanent placement for children with disabilities. Around the world, children with disabilities are often placed in institutions and left with little stimulation, care, or love. The project, currently being put in practice in over six countries, is designed to promote safe, nurturing family care for children out of parental care with a specific focus on children with disabilities (CWD). This includes supporting national care reforms for children in particular efforts towards family reunification, alternative family-based care, and influencing main stakeholders towards family care. With this project, ISS is promoting a safe, nurturing placement that amplifies the need for CWD to be protected and to receive the care and stimulation.

Overall, the CWD project aims for better protection of children with disabilities, including their safety, their future, and their rights to grow up with a family.

The Verona Principles

A few years ago, the ISS Professional Advisory Committee (PAC) heard about the sometimes devastating practice of surrogacy and the lack of guidelines involved. It was clear to the PAC that we needed to take a stand regarding the fact that none of the parties involved (women carrying the babies, the babies themselves, and the male donors) were being protected. In some instances, it was a free-for-all.

Surrogacy may be helpful when there is infertility and when couples are trying to create a child and family of their own. You may need a surrogate to carry a child or a donor to create an embryo, and surrogacy can be life-changing for many families. However, when the practice has no guidelines, no convention, and no best practice, it leaves everyone in a situation where basic human rights are forgotten and where children's rights are cast aside.

So, what does ISS do? The IRC took on the challenge of researching and writing. An initial five-page document quickly became a much larger paper once feedback was requested from professionals, from donors, from surrogates, and from donor-conceived individuals.

Thus were born the Verona Principles for the protection of the rights of the child born through surrogacy.[29] Anchored strongly on the Convention on the Rights of the Child, Verona Principles are designed for the protection of the rights of the child born through surrogacy and are developed in the expectation of complementary and evolving efforts in the wider human rights framework. With the hope that every state will want to implement the principles to better protect everyone involved in the practice of surrogacy, the Verona Principles promote the protection and rights of all involved.

Children on the move

In their daily work, ISS members work with children on the move. Our colleagues in Switzerland have built expertise regarding unaccompanied children on the move who were arriving in Europe. ISS Switzerland was developing initiatives, strategies, and case studies for assisting children on the move and exploring whether family reunification was possible. After many years of successful work, the expertise was expanded to the broader ISS network, and the idea was born of ISS developing a tool that would promote best practice when working with unaccompanied children and children on the move.

---

29. "Principles for the Protection of the Rights of the Child Born Through Surrogacy (Verona Principles)," (International Social Service, 2021), https://iss-ssi.org/storage/2023 /03/VeronaPrinciples_25February2021-1.pdf.

The aim was to provide a sustainable solution, a plan that would contribute to the better implementation of children's rights, notably reflected in the UN Convention on the Rights of the Child. The manual for the protection and safeguarding of children on the move is meant to help the work of professionals who are trying to protect these children who are at risk of neglect, abuse, exploitation, violence, illness, or worse. "This manual has been developed to encourage greater solidarity between countries when it comes to the integration (or reintegration) of children on the move, and to establish effective transnational systems for their protection."[30]

Equity in Permanency

The latest paper from ISS (2023) is one that was inspired by two studies led by two ISS members: ISS-USA and CFAB (ISS UK). After gathering interesting data in their respective countries on the issue of international kinship placement, the need for working principles in this area was born. How do we as an international network promote, support, and encourage more international kinship placements for children who can no longer be cared for by their biological parents?

It's easy! Inspired by the children's rights and common child protection practices, ISS set out to develop seven principles and best practice recommendations. The goal is to have every state adhere to the principles and put in practice the recommendations. Again, with the goal of wanting to protect children who can no longer be cared for by their parents, ISS was determined to offer solutions. Written by five members (UK, USA, Japan, Australia, and Canada) and with the strong collaboration of the IRC, the Equity in Permanency Principles[31] are a testament to what the ISS network can accomplish when it works together when it is determined to protect.

The ISS working group on Equity and Permanency is providing training on the principles and best practices. Equity in Permanency refers to principles of child protection practice that prioritise the exploration of

---

30. Jean Ayoub, "Children on the Move: From Protection Towards a Quality Sustainable Solution. A Practical Guide," (International Social Service, 2017): 5, https://iss-ssi.org/storage/2023/04/Childrenonthemove_EN.pdf.

31. "Equity in Permanency," (International Social Service, 2023), https://iss-ssi.org/storage/2023/08/ISS-Equity-in-Permanency-Aug-2023.pdf.

family placements, without discrimination of any kind, to achieve optimal long-term outcomes for the child.

The principles seek to empower child protection partners globally to have a child rights approach and promote policies and protocols that ensure all family placement options are explored for any child who can no longer be cared for by their parents. Furthermore, equity in permanency aims to access and connect with a child's extended family both locally and overseas to provide the best opportunity for them to be raised with a strong sense of identity, belonging, roots, and culture.

Equity in Permanency Seven Principles:

1. **Children's rights:** Every child has the right to know their family and to grow up in a home that is safe and loving. Once they can no longer be cared for by their birth parents, we need to make sure we can find an alternative that is in their best interest.
2. **Equal opportunities:** Every child deserves the same opportunity to be with family, regardless of where they are from, their race, their background, their religion, etc.
3. **Local expertise:** If we are going to be exploring families outside of our jurisdiction, we need to engage with local expertise in the other country – accredited professionals who can provide us with a clear insight about the community, services that are available, legal advice that we might require, and ongoing support to the family.
4. **No bias:** Child protection systems should work to address implicit and unconscious biases that may exist among key decision-makers regarding the complexities of transitioning a child into a family placement overseas and within a system that might differ from their own.
5. **Identity:** Child protection systems should prioritise a child's access to their culture, roots, language, extended family, community, and traditional land when making placement decisions. This approach respects the child's right to a robust family life and affords them the opportunity to maintain their identity.
6. **Adequate planning:** Child protection systems should always prepare a child for an impending placement with family members overseas through the development of a "Transition Plan" that includes consideration of preplacement support for carers to prepare for the

child's arrival, and local post placement follow-up and connection to resources.

7. **Accountability:** Child protection systems should seek to improve data collection, information management, and reporting systems related to children without parental care in all settings and situations to close existing data gaps and develop global and national baselines.

As you can see, the ISS network takes protection very seriously. This includes the protection of children, individuals, and families as well as the protection of rights, protection of identity, protection of culture, protection to feel safe, and the protection to be heard. When you lead with a determination to protect, you can achieve greatness for all. To protect and be protected – isn't this what we all want for ourselves, for others, for all?

Chapter 6: Consistency to Convince

Miglena Baldzhieva, Director of Intercountry Casework Department,
ISS-Bulgaria

Every day we find ourselves in situations where we try to persuade others of a different perspective to the one they currently hold. We aim to convince them that our approach or point of view is more appropriate in the circumstances. Convincing is a form of social influence encompassing change in beliefs, attitudes, and behaviours of people, which results from interpersonal interaction or from communications through intermediaries. Historically, convincing appeared to satisfy a certain public need related to the transition from a closed to an open society, which has seen the demise of tyrannical forms of government that excluded the participation of citizens in state administration. Democratic institutions have been erected, the most important of which are parliaments and courts.

In an open society, individuals are confronted with the need to think and to make decisions and compete with one another for social status. In such conditions, the need to convince emerges. Convincing is a model in which the addressee chooses whether to be influenced or not, in conditions of free choice. Therefore, to convince is not simply to induce or mislead somebody to perform certain actions. In contrast to coercion, deception, and manipulation, convincing shall be understood as a process, which requires the building of trust and in which the addressee is aimed at perceiving certain goals and ideas and taking specific actions for their realisation.

This chapter outlines the long journey and the consistent efforts of International Social Service-Bulgaria (ISS-Bulgaria) to convince authorities – and especially the courts – to use ISS as one of the mechanisms for international cooperation when children's rights and interests are affected in judicial proceedings.

In addition, the chapter explains how initial working relations were developed over several years and eventually turned into a stable partnership that opened space for crucial amendments to legislation, changes in case law, and the introduction of innovative approaches to guarantee the best interests of the child.

For 22 years now, ISS-Bulgaria has been part of the International Social Service family, which is currently represented in more than 120 countries and is a global actor in child protection, welfare, and uniting families across international borders since 1924.

In 2002, nobody in Bulgaria had heard of the International Social Service (ISS) or had any idea of how the ISS network could assist and support authorities by mediating between social services and the courts in different countries. That is why the first cross-border cases were referred to ISS-Bulgaria by our ISS partners and especially those from the European Union (EU) countries. These cases concerned mainly children who were victims of trafficking.

Our ISS partners requested social reports by the local child protection departments to determine whether it would be appropriate to return and reunite these children with their families in Bulgaria. Little by little, local child protection departments also started to approach our organisation by referring cases and requesting information from overseas to resolve family conflict situations and to ensure the protection of children in problematic cross-border situations.

It was only in 2005 that the courts in Bulgaria started to refer cases and began to request social reports from abroad for pending judicial proceedings. The reason for this was the requirement of the Child Protection Act that the judge request a social report in any judicial proceedings where the rights or interests of a child are affected.

At that time, many Bulgarians were already living and working abroad in the hope of a better life and an improvement in their well-being. Others entered into marriages with foreign citizens, their children were born abroad, and then, in turn, some of them separated. They then turned to the Bulgarian courts to resolve disputes regarding the children, mainly related to parental responsibility, a child's residence after the parents' separation, contact with the nonresident parent, and the payment of child maintenance.

This was also the time when many parents left Bulgaria while their children stayed in the care of their grandparents and extended families. These parents were looking for opportunities to reunite with their children and take them overseas, which required a judicial decision to resolve the situation. In these and many other cases, judges sought ways to obtain information about the situation of the child or his parents abroad so that they could make a decision in the child's best interests.

At the same time, Bulgaria was not yet a full member of the European Union, and the opportunities offered by the EU regulations as international legal instruments could not be used in our country. The mechanisms for cooperation and exchange of information regulated by the Hague Conventions were not well known to legal professionals, and very few of them sought assistance from the central authorities regarding cases with an international element. There was no experience with the Hague Network of Judges.

The realities were such that many of the disputes in court were decided without the availability of information from abroad, which could have assisted the judge as to the child's best interests in the particular situation.

In the beginning, our work with the courts was difficult and hugely challenging. During the first years of cooperation, we were handling only a few court cases annually, as judges were rather skeptical about seeking our assistance.

A significant breakthrough came at the end of 2009, when ISS-Bulgaria, in partnership with the German branch of ISS and with the financial support of the Federal Ministry of Family Affairs, Senior Citizens, Women and Youth in Germany, organised an international conference in Sofia titled, "The best interests of the child in family conflicts with an international element: Opportunities for cooperation and assistance from the International Social Service in searching and finding a solution."

We wanted to present to the professional communities in Bulgaria, and especially to the legal community, the work of ISS as a network, the possibilities for cooperation with courts and social services, as well as the practice of the ISS-Bulgaria since it was set up in 2002. Initially only two judges responded to our invitation and came to the conference. Shortly before the start of the conference, however, I was invited to give an interview on the Bulgarian national radio, when I announced that a German family judge would take a special part in the conference, and she would share her experience and the assistance she seeks and receives from the German branch of International Social Service. Two hours after my interview, the conference hall was full of judges from different courts in Sofia who had heard my interview on the radio.

It was extremely encouraging for them to hear from their colleague, Judge Verena Clausen-Schmidt from the District Court Berlin, how she works with ISS. In particular, she explained why she requests assistance from our colleagues in Berlin and how she receives social reports from abroad providing authentic information about the child or his parents who are outside Germany, which helps her to make a judgment in the best interests of the child.

This conference was a turning point for our work with the courts. Since then, requests for assistance coming from judges began to increase significantly. Our assistance was sought by judges not only from Sofia, but also from courts across the country. The provision of social reports from our partners around the globe raised the confidence of the judicial system, and we were soon working on an average of 50 cases with the courts annually.

Our good cooperation with the courts created space for other initiatives, one of which was known as "Roadshows" for judges and social workers. The Roadshows were aimed at training judges how to apply the best interests of the child principle enshrined in the UN Convention on the Rights of the Child and the Bulgarian Child Protection Act 2000. When the latter had been adopted, judges encountered difficulties in applying this principle into their daily work. When they were invited to forums and conferences, the most persistent question amongst them was, "How can we know what is in the best interests of a child?"

It was not easy to explain, and in seeking a solution, ISS-Bulgaria proposed a new way forward, which was inspired by Judge Nick Crichton from the United Kingdom. He was the one to suggest we set up Roadshows, whereby we visit judges, social workers, and other child-focused professionals across Bulgaria in their own towns and help them to establish a multidisciplinary way of working. He proposed including Mrs. Gill Timmis, an experienced English social worker, to deliver seminars with him so that together they could demonstrate the UK model of a judge and a social worker working together in the best interests of children.

As a result, ISS-Bulgaria organised and financed the first Roadshow, making presentations and discussing practice with professionals involved in judicial proceedings concerning children, including children in cross-border situations. Over the years, the Roadshows became an event in Bulgaria, and legal and social care professionals would keenly await the Roadshow arriving in their locality. For five years, all twenty-eight court centres in Bulgaria were covered. We held thirty-two seminars involving 830 professionals, of which 256 were judges and 387 social workers. Participants were especially impressed by the English "welfare checklist" as a tool to assist professionals to collect and analyse information to better understand the situation of the child. As a result, there was then a demand for a similar checklist to be included in the Bulgarian legislation.

Luckily, at that time, the legislators were discussing amendments to the Child Protection Act. I was invited to join a working group, where I had the opportunity to explain the welfare checklist, how it assisted professionals in England to make decisions regarding children, and how Bulgarian judges needed a similar tool to streamline their work involving children. As a consequence of our Roadshow initiative, in 2009, the welfare checklist was introduced with some minor amendments to the Child Protection Act.

However, this was just a small step ahead as many other challenges still remained. We at ISS-Bulgaria hoped to keep the fire of progress burning before the Roadshows came to an end. Based on the feedback and recommendations of the participants, we prepared the next stage, calling it the "Child-friendly justice" programme.

Our purpose was to ensure more effective protection of children's rights by developing and introducing standards underpinning child-friendly justice. In 2012, our organisation selected three Model Courts and fifteen Satellite Courts, where judges and social workers were willing to work hard to change the way children were treated in civil judicial proceedings, including those with an international element. For three years, our team trained sixteen judges and social workers, with whom we drafted twelve standards that would guarantee children's rights before, during, and after the court proceedings. Good practices were developed for the application of these standards showing how they were working in the courts and the social services. These standards allowed ISS-Bulgaria to pilot and introduce innovative services such as the Separated Parents Information Programme, the Parenting Plan, and Child Contact Centres, to which judges referred children and parents to help them resolve the conflict situation.

Inspired by Judge Crichton's courtroom at the Inner London Family Proceedings Court, eight courts in Bulgaria adapted their premises for the needs of the children that are interviewed in judicial proceedings. Seeking cooperation by judges from the ISS global network was described as a good practice under one of the principles.[32]

---

32. Miglena Baldzhieva, "Child-Friendly Justice. Standards for Children in Civil Law Matters. Good Practices," (International Social Service - Bulgaria, 2015): 115–117, https://www.iss-bg.org/pic/Child-friendly_justice_book.pdf.

At the same time, case law regarding judicial proceedings involving children and families in cross-border situations was also changing due to two key court decisions of the Supreme Court of Cassation issued in 2018[33] and 2019.[34] The first one concerned a mother who decided to move to Spain with her child. She filed an application to the first-instance court for relocation of the child, but the judge rejected her application. She appealed the judgment, but the second-instance court confirmed the refusal.

The case went to the Supreme Court of Cassation. In the motives of its judgment, the Supreme Court of Cassation pointed out that, in considering the claims, the right of the child to reside in the Kingdom of Spain and to have the residence there with his mother was denied. Instead, the court should have assessed how the mother's declared intention to settle down in the Kingdom of Spain, assessed as serious, could affect the child's interests and the possibility of maintaining a full relationship with each of the parents, and what would be the impact of this circumstance on the wishes and feelings of the child; his physical, mental, and emotional needs; and the consequences for him.

In view of this, the Supreme Court of Cassation underlined in its decision that when considering the case, the courts did not show due activity and did not request a social report as to receive information regarding the living conditions in the home of the applicant and did not collect evidence to ensure the health and educational needs of the child, which is considered as evidentiary incompleteness and determines a substantial violation of the rules of judicial procedure.

The court should have ordered the preparation of a social report by the social services in the relevant locality in Spain as to establish the circumstances relevant to the assessment of the best interests of the child and, more specifically, the parenting capacity of the mother. This would include the domestic and social conditions in which the child will be raised in the Kingdom of Spain as well as the care of the child. The court should have directed the mother to determine how the child's health and educational needs would be met.

---

33. Supreme Court of Cassation of the Republic of Bulgaria, Decision No. 34, (Sofia, 2018): https://www.vks.bg/pregled-akt.jsp?type=ot-delo&id=BDFD38272849F73CC2258257004BC869.

34. Supreme Court of Cassation of the Republic of Bulgaria, Decision No. 207, (Sofia, 2019): https://www.vks.bg/pregled-akt.jsp?type=ot-delo&id=06A383B3C7AAF880C22584D2002B3735.

In view of this, the Supreme Court of Cassation overturned the judgment and sent back the case to the second-instance court for a new examination by another panel of judges. Pursuant to the instructions of the Supreme Court of Cassation, the judges from the second-instance court requested assistance from ISS-Bulgaria. When we provided the court with the requested social report with the assistance of our ISS colleagues from Spain, the court granted the mother's request to relocate the child.

Despite these achievements, in 2017, ISS-Bulgaria was confronted with the biggest challenge ever regarding our cooperation with the courts. In particular, we were in danger of having our intercountry work suspended and also in danger of significant financial sanctions. In April 2017, Sofia Regional Court, the largest first-instance court in the country, requested assistance from ISS-Bulgaria for providing a social report from Dubai in judicial proceedings regarding a dispute between separated parents. The parents were arguing regarding the future of their son around issues such as the child's residence, the exercise of parental rights, contacts between the child and the nonresident parent, and the child's monthly maintenance payments.

The mother and the child were Bulgarians and were residing in Bulgaria, whereas the father was Lebanese and working in Dubai, where the family previously lived. The child was in-vitro conceived in Canada, where the parents were initially living. Our partners in Dubai provided us with the requested social report explaining the father's situation in the emirate, which we forwarded to the court. This information helped the judge make her decision granting the father a relatively broad regime of contacts and personal relations with his son in Bulgaria.

Dissatisfied with the judgment, the mother complained to the Personal Data Protection Commission, claiming violation of the personal data protection legislation and especially the newly introduced General Data Protection Regulation known as GDPR. She was arguing that ISS-Bulgaria transferred sensitive personal data to a third country outside the EU without her consent and without permission of the Personal Data Protection Commission. The Commission, in turn, referred the mother's complaint to the Inspectorate of the Supreme Judicial Council to decide whether the court could refer to our organisation and to request provision of a social report from overseas, especially from the United Arab Emirates.

The Inspectorate sent back the complaint to the Commission, explaining that it did not have powers to make a decision regarding the processing of personal data by ISS-Bulgaria, which is a legal entity and not a court. The Commission eventually concluded that in providing the court with a social report from Dubai, our organisation did not violate the personal data protection legislation.

The mother appealed the decision of the Commission to the Administrative Court, but her appeal was rejected. In his motives, the administrative judge argued that "in this case, given the correspondence exchanged between the Court and ISS-Bulgaria, it should be assumed that the provision of the personal data to a legal entity in the United Arab Emirates was made by order and instruction of a Court for the performance of a task in the interest of justice, which is unquestionably in the public interest. The personal data including sensitive personal data, included in the application to the Court, the response to the application, the birth certificate and evidences in the case, reproduced by International Social Service-Bulgaria in the so-called Case note, has been transferred to a third country outside the European Union, for the protection of rights under a Court order in pending judicial proceedings, and in fulfillment of an instruction of a public body – a Court, which has assessed in advance the necessary data for the performance of the assigned task. In view of this, the Administrative Court shared the conclusion of the Commission that the transfer of personal data took place on the basis of the legislation, i.e., the contested decision of the Commission was made in accordance with the substantive data protection law and the purpose of the law."[35]

The mother used her last option and appealed the judgment to the Supreme Administrative Court. The supreme judges confirmed the judgment and resolved the dispute with a final court decision. The decision of the Supreme Administrative Court confirmed the practice that judges can freely seek assistance from ISS-Bulgaria and receive information from the ISS global network that can help them make decisions in the best interests of the child involved in cross-border judicial proceedings.

At present, it can be said that the path we have taken and the struggles we have waged over the years have been filled with ups and downs, efforts and

---

35. Administrative Court of the City of Sofia, Decision No. 4842, (Sofia, 2022): https:// search-sofia-adms-g.justice.bg/Acts/GetActContent?BlobID=2ad8db51-c421-4490 -a9a7-057497000d2e.

challenges of various natures. However, by setting clear goals, developing good practices, eliminating distractions, investing time and resources, establishing trust, and staying accountable, we at the International Social Service-Bulgaria passed all the tests and stayed consistent in convincing others – courts, authorities, social services, lawyers, parents, and ISS colleagues around the globe.

Now it is time to celebrate our successes as this journey has made us what we are today: an organisation that has a well-established reputation in Bulgaria and is known as a body of uncontested competence, which is in line with what has been said about the ISS network in the Explanatory Report under the 1996 Hague Convention.[36]

Everything that has been described can be summarised with the words of Judge Genoveva Ilieva: "My work as a judge obliges me to guarantee and to protect to the fullest extent the children's interests when they are involved in judicial proceedings. I am required to collect evidence on my own, including social reports from overseas, when it comes to cross-border cases, which I have been able to do with the assistance of the International Social Service-Bulgaria. I do appreciate collaboration with the ISS network as it gives me a sense of security that what is reflected in the social report corresponds to the circumstances of the child and above all, it helps me to make a decision in accordance with the best interests of the that particular child."

---

36. In his Explanatory Report on the Convention of 19 October 1996 on Jurisdiction, Applicable Law, Recognition, Enforcement and Co-operation in Respect of Parental Responsibility and Measures for the Protection of Children, Paul Lagarde defines International Social Service as a body of "such uncontested competence" toward the Central authority would have recourse (HCCH Publications, 1996), p, 591: https://www.hcch.net/pt/publications-and-studies/details4/?pid=2943.

Chapter 7: Capacity to Educate

Jacqueline Pascarl OAM, International Social Service Governing Board member

Education is not only the acquisition of knowledge, it is the insight facilitated by exposure to new concepts; it is mental muscle memory and rote learning. Education is the window to empathy and self-determination, the most unassailable edifice of mental strength and autonomy of thought. Through education, we expose ourselves to concepts and debate, to controls and freedoms afforded by dissemination of positional thinking and liberation. Education is the key to the most powerful position in the world – information. However, information, in and of itself, is nigh useless without the ability to distill and discern facts and understand reasoning and debate. Education is also the precept of search and striving for larger vistas, or conversely, defining the world around us within boundaries made from an informed position and juxtaposition of the physical and the conceptual reality of our own existence. It could also be said that observation, either by coincidence or circumstance, is an effective means of education as well.

Family is the very portal of learning and education. The smile, the touch, the kind word, or soothing murmur as an infant's head is cradled against the breast form us as humans and create the basis of all our further educative endeavours and vistas.

Family is resilience for most people. Without family and the succor of safety, familiarity, and love, resilience is nigh impossible to achieve. Resilience cannot only be defined by the ability to regroup, move on, and bounce back, it is also the ability to redefine, flourish, and pass on life lessons to others. Children need a family unit to blossom and reach their fullest potential. Resilience is at the heart of the human condition, but how we evince resilience as humans also depends on the state of the human psyche. And nothing is more damaging to the human psyche in its formative years of childhood than the separation of child from family and the severing of familial bonds.

The importance of the family unit, which can define, shape, and nurture an individual, was presciently and intuitively recognised by the founders of International Social Service in 1924 (originally known as International Migration Service) as they began to build the foundations of an organisation that would go on to work in scores of countries around the globe.

Family reunification, the necessity for which is caused by the movement, forced or voluntary, across borders of large groups of peoples, fleeing conflict, natural disaster, or economic repression and hopelessness, became a focal point of our founders' work. So, too, the involuntary cleaving of families caught up in the circumstances of fractured domestic units, relationship breakdowns, or geopolitical struggles necessitated or eventuated in upheavals and refugee movements over porous borders or almost insurmountable oceans.

One hundred years on, we must pay tribute to the prescient forethought that the women founders of ISS gave to realising that true resilience can only come from a sound sense of self, and the seeds of this vital, internalised human power will, ultimately, take root in the formative childhood years amidst a stable family unit.

Stability takes many forms of definition depending on cultural mores. To some, it is food at regular times a day, a certainty of nourishment against hunger, and availability of medical care; in others, we include shelter, education, access to clean water, and safety – both mental and physical. But the absolute touchstone of stability is uninterrupted nurturing in a family unit, in whatever iteration our respective societies deem acceptable to view that unit and proffer recognition.

The commonality of humanity is simple though. We birth children into what we hope will be a safe environment; we feed, nurture, educate, and love those children; we instill values and empathy; and the stability of both family and location, of identity and example, are woven into the fabric of those children's lives and provide a safety net of comfort and life lessons from which to draw. These lessons in the vagaries of life and the boundaries of existence are both emotional and psychological. They form the basis of adulthood and the ability to navigate challenges and meet obstacles with adaptation – that is resilience in its truest form.

ISS has recognised this genesis of resilience since its inception in 1924, protecting and reuniting children, individuals, and families separated by international borders. ISS has worked with governments, the League of Nations (later the United Nations), nongovernment organisations (NGOs), intergovernmental agencies, and private citizens with like-minded ideals to focus on the needs of children and families amidst wars, genocides, adoptions, surrogacy, abductions and divorce, and devastating natural and man-made disasters. That main focus of ISS is reunification, and the healing of relationships is the foundation of resilience and stability.

A core principle holds tight to ISS envisioning a world where the rights of children, families, and individuals are recognised, protected, supported, and defended in all situations of either voluntary or forced migration. Underpinning this value is the belief that our world should see people safe, protected, and supported without discrimination of any kind, and where children have an inalienable right to a safe environment that supports positive emotional and intellectual development of well-being and a strong sense of belonging, which can only lead to resilience in its truest form. Self-identity, the accumulation of a strong sense of self, the "id" in the evolution of self-awareness from the cradle to the grave, or self-determination and decision-making, begins from family connection and leads to resilience and independent thought process. The protection of the dignity of all human beings and their human rights defines ISS's professional integrity and the championing of social justice across 120 countries around the world.

The complexities and importance of family reunification can never be understated or underestimated. Not all cases have a storybook happy ending, but resilience of the human spirit and the determination of humanity to know one's own family are always at the core of any scenario in this field of endeavour and the driving force in the majority of humankind. As such, ISS has made this a driver of its social work and its focus – to bring families back together and to provide children with their identity and place in the world through this reunification despite often insurmountable scenarios.

I am one of the current crop of women to be a Governor of ISS. I sit on the ISS Governing Board and have been a board member since 2023. I follow humbly in the hallowed footprints of the collective humanitarian tour de force of Suzanne "Lili" Ferriere (Switzerland), Lady Dorothy Gladstone (Britain), Mary E. Hurlbutt (USA), and Ruth Larned, and scores of others who understood the world from quiet observation and fact collection, along with self-education and plain hard work at the coal face of human suffering and desperation. They were women of vision, who had witnessed, at close quarters, the devastation and aftermath of World War One. They all believed that the breaking of family ties by virtue of borders, or distance caused by forced or voluntary migration, created a new form of suffering that was vital to recognise in a modern society. This was the momentum and guiding core principle that has always informed ISS's work and raison d'etre. Alongside the formidable but deceptively all female YWCA (Young Women's Christian Association) in the USA and that organisation's International Division, women began to emerge from the shadows of being perceived as nonvoting citizens and docile domestic and espoused helpmates to a power to be recognised and heard for their insights and innovations.

To quote author Roxana Banu in a chapter of *Portraits of Women in International Law* (2023):

"Since 1924, ISS has helped millions of families navigate complex socio-legal problems as a result of migration. Women were the lifeblood of this organisation from the very beginning: setting the vision, raising funds across all branches, lobbying a male-dominated international scene in Geneva, London, and New York, and leading transnational research teams at the intersection of private international law and international social work. The conventional historiographies of public and private international law (PrIL) fail to record both the ISS's unique perspective in the international law arena as a social work organisation and the pioneering work of its female actors in many transnational socio-legal projects." [37]

My own association with ISS harks back to the late 1990s when I was asked to discuss the impact of international parental child abduction at a conference in Melbourne, Australia, at which a more recently established branch of ISS was participating in an international forum. I could see, as I interacted with ISS members in discussion groups, that an alternative negotiating opportunity, provided by well-educated social workers from within a global network, made eminent sense as an addition to the current norm of adversarial legal pursuance and prosecution. Harnessing the resources and network of ISS in this highly fraught world of lost children, cross-cultural difficulties, and heightened emotions would be a valuable addition to the field of child abduction and language barriers that were routinely encountered in the fora of reunification and welfare of the child victim.

At the time, I was CEO and founder of The Empty Arms Network of Australia and had also consulted to and advised the European Union, Lord

---

37. Roxana Banu, "Forgotten Female Actors in Private International Law," in *Portraits of Women in International Law*, ed. Immi Tallgren (Oxford University Press, 2023): 276.

Chancellor's Department in the United Kingdom, Australia's Department of Foreign Affairs, and the US State Department in the field of the highly specialised sphere of Hague Convention and international parental child abduction. I had made documentary films on the topic, written books, and won awards for my work in the field, yet the irony of my situation was not lost on me. I was an unwilling expert; my path to this role, to becoming recognised on the global stage as an expert in this field of tragedy, anguish, conundrums, heartbreak, and bitter family disputes, was an evolution of circumstance and not one of choice.

The expertise I had garnered to enable me to speak on these specific topics had come via research, self-education, interaction, observation, experience, and advocacy. It had been reached not only from study, but from personal, firsthand experience, for I was both within a category of global statistics, that of parental child abduction, and of advocacy, having become an initially unwilling advocate and champion for parents around the world who had lost their child/children to child abduction across borders. As the term suggests, *parental child abduction* is the scenario where, upon the demise of an intimate relationship, one parent illegally removes the progeny of the marriage to another country without the permission of the other parent and, in most cases, without warning, acting precipitously and outside of legal bounds. Quite often there is a history of domestic violence involved, which heightens the concern for the abducted child. It is quite routine for the left-behind parent to be denied any form of contact with the abducted child and any sort of information as to their well-being and welfare. The scenarios can often be diverse, but the commonality of loss and devastation, of despair and panic, are all too common, no matter the language or location of those parents left behind. The crime of abduction, of the unilateral abrogation of parental rights, cuts across all socioeconomic strata and across gender; although there is a slight tilt towards more abductors being male, parents of both sexes do undertake this cruel crime.

When it happened to my young children on the 9th of July, 1992, I literally went from reading the news to being the news in the space of twelve hours. I was a recognised face on television, a creature of the airwaves with a radio show and on-screen time bringing major investigative stories to the public. The abduction of my children aged seven and nine – a daughter named Shahirah and a son named Iddin – made headlines around my own country, Australia, but also around the world, for it involved all the elements of a newspaper and ratings juggernaut. I was a television broadcaster appearing on the prime-time news nightly, but until the kidnapping of my children, no one had known outside of my closest family and friends that I was also a former royal princess (by marriage). The abductor was my former husband, a favoured grandson of the King of Malaysia from whom I had been divorced for seven years prior to him kidnapping our children from their long-term residence with me in Australia – where the children and I had settled after our marriage ended years before. I was an Australian-born woman, and the children had held Australian citizenship since birth. We had lived quietly and undisturbed with the legal consent of my former husband until he had decided to run for political office and needed a way to catapult his public profile from Playboy Prince to solid and avenging father, erroneously using his religion as justification for a kidnapping.

I remember the devastation of having my children ripped without warning from their beds, from my life, and from their community. I recall vividly the joy of celebrating my daughter's seventh birthday one day and then the agonising desperation of holding her pillow to my tear-sodden face just a day later, in an attempt to capture her scent in a visceral moment of grief. I can still see in my mind's eye our whimpering dog laying her head on my foot as I sobbed uncontrollably on my nine-year-old son's bed – I was a crushed bundle of despair and anguish at their loss and the battle ahead that was unfolding.

As I close my eyes, I see an image of myself from my memories of 1992. I stand before the mirror in my bathroom, dripping from the shower where I had sought refuge and momentary privacy from the television cameras and the photographers at the front door, from the police investigators in my living room, the federal agents on phone tracing, and the constant chiming of the phones outside the door of the bathroom and the satellite dishes and broadcast vans on the verge outside the house. There I took stock of what ten days post abduction had brought: A skeletal woman looked back at me from the mirror, stress-induced vomiting had taken a toll, dark circles ringed my eyes, and small bald patches had begun to show, as clumps of hair had begun to drop out from my scalp and onto my pillow, even as sleep had evaded me for days, and an aching grief and exhaustion buried itself into my bones and shuddered me awake whenever I closed my eyes. My hands shook uncontrollably as I attempted to swipe my face clear in the mirror and prepare myself for another day of media barrage and legal battles along with political lobbying and diplomatic maneuvering by my government and that of Malaysia.

I remember the sensation of a giant apple corer being taken to my soul and removing my essence as a mother, and the deep visceral pain of worrying how my small children were coping with strangers and a foreign language, how they were eating and sleeping, what they thought I had allowed to happen to them. They had never been apart from me since their birth and hardly knew their biological father as he had continued to live in Malaysia, nine hours away by plane, and saw them only every eighteen months for a few days at a time (his choice), as he had remarried and had another large family. But my children were his eldest. And I was a foreigner. Their kidnap was violent and terrifying; hired muscle from the human trafficking trade and child prostitution were used to carry out the plan. My small children, I eventually discovered, were drugged and separated, transported as parcels in vehicles driven at high speed to evade police and a nationwide search. It was a clandestine operation over several days in utility trucks, with driving routes from one end of a very vast Australia to another. Eventually my defenceless children were bundled aboard a leaking fishing vessel, which stalled mid-ocean in the treacherous waters off Indonesia's Irian Jaya. The kidnapping included SOS pleas for a maritime rescue and the involvement of the Indonesian military governor of the backwater province . . . and guns, lots of guns. After twenty-five days on the run, the children and my former husband, Prince Bahrin, surfaced in Malaysia during which my erstwhile prince called his actions "jihad" during a press conference and launched his political campaign as a newly minted fundamentalist candidate for election. Apparently jihad was now a war to be waged against children – his own.

How would my children cope? What effect was this violent, terrifying, and horrific abduction to have on my seven- and nine-year-old children? Did they remember me, and what psychological tortures did they have to endure in order to conform to their new lives, language, and environment? Who, if anyone, was comforting them when they woke crying for me at night? How much damage was being done to their fragile and immature psyches?

I was to wait almost two decades to find these answers from them, my lost children, for that is the duration of time they were held incommunicado from me, no letters, no phone calls – just silence, or the occasional staged and distressing appearance in the media as shadowy punctuation notes of a political aspirant father making collateral polling booth fodder of our children.

I was not to see them again in a torturous time frame that spanned across the waning and waxing of two centuries. I was not to know that their brainwashing was to be so inculcated as to render their emotional and sociological identities so ruptured and distorted that we were to be strangers in so many ways when I met them as the adults they became.

I have vivid recollections of what it was like to sit in a park in the rain, fourteen months after their abduction, a razor blade in my hand tickling my wrist with its sharp edge and drawing small globules of blood, contemplating my suicide and the blissful release from a media circus my demise would bring for my children and the sweet release from my own pain. But I snapped out of my morbid toying with the blade as I heard the squeal of a small child in another part of the park: "mummy, mummy," the cry rang out into the space around me. The realisation that I would not be around for Iddin and Shahirah were they to make it back to me and what the consequences of my self-indulgence would mean for my children was too much to be explained by strangers. Violently, I flung the razor away, shook my head, and slowly got to my knees.

I chose life and existence.

RESILIENCE – whether sought or unbidden – can be quite a shocking revelation.

For me, this was the first bounce-back of resiliency and clear-headedness. It was to bring me to another place in my mind and my career. Advocacy, and the acquisition of knowledge and education – it became my one hope for sanity. Over the days and weeks that followed, I indulged my grief in strict rations, taking to my bed weeping only after accomplishing a certain amount of tasks: public press conferences calling on political leaders to assist my children, telephone calls to diplomats or unionists, back-to-back meetings with my legal advisors, discussions with experts in international law around the world, and then one more element entered – other left-behind parents seeking their children.

And so began the rest of my life, one structured around educating myself in international law, in foreign treaties and diplomatic relations, sovereign law, and most importantly in advocacy. This chosen, but also accidental, path was to bring me into the sphere of negotiation and legal dealings. It fostered a burning desire in me to reunite other families, as each of the 490 children I was to work on bringing home to a left-behind parent over the next seventeen years was one tiny brick of hope that someday, I would hold my own children again.

However, challenges are something that I thrive on, and so, after a very diverse breadth of experience in child abduction advocacy and having made an award-winning film on the topic, I wanted to also diversify my abilities and to fill my life so much that I simply had only a pinpoint of life, or downtime, that would allow me time to grieve and fight for my children. So, I went to work in conflict and disaster zones, operating in refugee camps and reuniting families, finding answers and solutions to tragedy and necessity. I worked in Africa building schools, and later, in war-torn Bosnia and Kosovo amidst the seething mass of human distress and injury and the tattered remains of families and lost people. I retrained, finding my niche in disaster management and humanitarian response. I got a truck license so I could run aid convoys and build havens for the lost, but mostly, I truly found myself and an identity adjacent to being a mother. I learnt to use my language skills and my former title as princess for a more common good. I grew bold; I had no compunction in buttonholing presidents and prime ministers, judges, billionaires, celebrities, and politicians around the globe to achieve better outcomes for refugees, the disenfranchised, and the lost and stolen. For in truth, until my fuller life could be restored, I needed to channel my energies into others and survive a very new reality. Working in disaster zones, in East Timor, Turkey, New Zealand, Australia, Rwanda, or Indonesia, gave me a purpose. The privilege of proffering practical solutions and helping others reunite safely with their families and loved ones has been the mainstay of my mind's health and my raison d'etre. But mostly, it has been the hope of our commonality of humanity and love, of the human spirit and its resilience, that has seen me through cancer, kidnap, death, and despair.

Resiliency should not be confused with tenacity or obstinacy, as they are entirely different conditions and mindsets. Resilience is defined by the ability to lift oneself up, to endure, to proceed forward even when dealt the harshest of blows. Resilience is to not take bitterness forward in life's journey, but to forge beyond life's setbacks and find or create positivity and possibilities for oneself amidst a nugget of self-doubt or an overarching exhaustion in which one could choose to drown. Resilience is the rubberised, stubborn core of id, or one's soul and life experience that provides the courage to reassemble one's beaten or broken heart and rise to the surface of an ocean of despair and gasp for air, striking for the shore as a natural instinctive belief in a better moment to come. Hope for fleeting moments, and the hope of another try, another opportunity to see joy, feel love or connection, or triumph, even in tiny increments, that is true resilience and the essence of what is provisioned to us when we have the benefit of family bonds and our own unshakeable identity. These possibilities of self-identity and of a hope for all families and all children to know one another and form the values and memories that sustain them into resilience are why I work with ISS on the Governing Board, and why I will always strive to educate, advocate, and reunite children with their families across borders and oceans. We are humanity, in its often cruel, seething, and messy divisions, but that does not mean humanity should give in to hopelessness and accept geopolitical divisions, or place these conundrums in the "too hard" basket. Our future is in our children. They are the hope for our very survival and the unification of humanity which depends on our commonality. We all love our children in the same way no matter our race, religion, or geography, and that is our truest resilience. For resilience is hope shaped into a form of the human spirit that remains unassailable, yet damaged and repaired. Resilience is a wholeness of self with the oft-bruising experience of life, along with all the future possibilities of potential and insight.

ISS has always recognised the necessity of building resilience through education and the reunification of families as the true building blocks for a strong global society. It is with this learned foresight and determination that we face the coming hundred years of the work ahead as we look back with humility and gratitude to the women pioneers who carved a new global understanding of social work, family cohesion, and humanitarian reunification. It is my hope that I can add to this immense body of achievement in some small way and help steer this international confederation of member states towards the next hundred years of hope.

Chapter 8: Resilience to Overcome

Carolyn Housman, CEO, ISS UK (Children and Families Across Borders)

The origins of ISS: Forged in resilience

As noted throughout the book, the genesis of the International Social Service (ISS) network is a tale of resilience, determination, and unwavering dedication amidst turbulent times. We can trace the origins of ISS directly back to 1855. In that year in London, two women independently decided to do something to help vulnerable women who were far from home, and they focused on two groups in particular: nurses travelling to or from the battlefield hospitals of Turkey and the Crimea, and the large numbers of young single women travelling to the cities in search of work.

Mary Jane Kinnaird established the London Young Women's Institute, for Nightingale's nurses and other working women, with residential accommodation at the North London Home on Charlotte Street. Later she opened other boarding houses near ports and railway stations so that travelling women could have somewhere cheap and safe to stay. Meanwhile, also in 1855, Emma Robarts set up a Prayer Union in Barnet, London, which she later called the Christian Association of Young Women, with the purpose of not just praying with and for young women, but also offering help in a number of practical ways.

The two women met in 1877 and together formed the Young Women's Christian Association (YWCA). This was to be in line with the YMCA, which had been founded in 1844. Meanwhile, in the US, similar groups were established in Boston and New York in the 1860s, and by the 1890s, there were branches in several other countries.

By 1920, a World's YWCA had been formed and convened at Champéry in Switzerland. Delegates recognised the need for coordinated action between countries to ease the passage of those travelling to unfamiliar lands and to reduce the number of migrants being refused entry to the country to which they had gone. It was decided to establish a Standing Committee on Migration in 1921, based in London, and to set up a thorough study of the situation and establish methods of coordination of effort.

An American social worker with US YWCA, Mary E. Hurlbutt was commissioned to do a six-month survey of migration from Germany, Poland, Czechoslovakia, France, and Switzerland. Her seminal report, "The Welfare of Migrants," was published in 1921. It highlighted the enormous problems for migrants: lack of resources, lack of information, confusion, desperation, and exploitation. It made a strong case for the greater protection of migrants. Not only did this report inform the work of all branches of the World's YWCA, but it was also put before the International Emigration Commission set up by the International Labour Office (ILO) and so reached a wider audience. Mary Hurlbutt later became Director of ISS from 1926 to 1930.

In 1923, the Migration Committee of the World's YWCA recognised the need for a permanent programme. The YWCA had been founded by Protestants, and although its work was always nondiscriminatory, it was perceived in some countries as being biased. So, it was decided to set up an independent and internationally governed organisation. There was some discussion about putting the new organisation directly under the auspices of the League of Nations, or under the Emigration Section of the International Labour Office, but in the end, it was decided that it would have more freedom if it was completely independent.

In May 1924, at a meeting of the World's YWCA in Washington, DC, the decision of the Migration Committee was ratified, and on the 1st of October 1924, the International Migration Service (IMS) was established. Although this remained the official name of the organisation until 1946, the first mention of the name as International Social Service was at a meeting of the Committee in September 1924, and this name soon came into common usage.

Despite the good intentions, resources were limited after the First World War, and the IMS teetered on the brink of financial abyss. Yet, undeterred by the daunting odds, the founding women formed "the committee on the universe" and began to fundraise in their spare time. They pooled their own meagre resources but found they barely had enough to survive for one week. An appeal to a philanthropic foundation brought enough funds for a further three months. Using every possible contact, they gradually built up a support base and raised enough to carry on.

The records show that there were many times when ISS branches around the world demonstrated resilience and determination to overcome the odds. At times, it looked as though the service would not be able to continue. Many pleas came from international and national organisations to keep going because the service was much appreciated, and so, with salary cuts and other retrenchments, somehow every crisis was survived.

Wartime resilience in France

The story of the ISS French branch during the Second World War is one of resilience and ingenuity in the face of extreme adversity. When German forces occupied Paris, they seized the ISS office, leaving no time to destroy sensitive records. Françoise Vignat, however, courageously eluded the guards and reclassified records of Jewish clients under a less conspicuous category. Returning later, she managed to convince occupying forces that ISS work was apolitical, allowing limited operations to continue, even in tandem with the German Red Cross. Funding these efforts required creativity: the branch president smuggled money into Paris by concealing it in her knitting wool.

As the war progressed, ISS shifted operations to Lyon, facilitating the emigration of Jewish children to Switzerland. Ms. Trillat, who later led the branch, was arrested, imprisoned, and tortured but survived until the war's end.

Postwar, the French branch took on significant responsibilities, including assisting nationals from countries lacking representation in France, supporting the repatriation of French citizens, and caring for displaced children – such as 1,200 French children in Switzerland and 900 Polish children separated from their families.

By the war's end, four branches remained operational: France, Italy, Switzerland, and the US. Though the French branch reopened, others in Germany and Greece soon after, some – like those in Czechoslovakia and Poland – could not resume. This cooperation among branches proved vital in supporting countless displaced families.

Inception in the UK and enduring challenges

In the UK, a similar challenge was encountered. ISS UK (originally ISS GB) was founded just after the Second World War, in 1955, and achieved recognition as a charitable entity by British authorities in 1956. The first director was a formidable woman, Kay Luce, who remained at the helm of the charity for twenty years. Even then, she did not disappear but joined the Council and remained on it until 1982. She was then appointed as vice president until her death in 2003 at almost 101 years old.

ISS UK faced hurdles in providing services, especially in generating assessment reports for referrals from overseas. Previously, these referrals were directed to voluntary or statutory social work agencies, yet reluctance to undertake unpaid work arose with the normalisation of service charges.

World Refugee Year

Throughout the 1950s, there was growing concern about the sheer number of refugees in the world, resulting in chronically overloaded systems. Other solutions had to be found, and the idea for a World Refugee Year came from two British MPs – Chris Chataway and Timothy Raison – together with a couple of journalists. There were three main aims: 1) to arouse the conscience of the world, 2) to collect funds, and 3) to assist in designing permanent solutions for refugees. Their concern was for three groups in particular: first, the estimated 162,000 still in postwar refugee camps in Europe; second, the 915,000 Palestinian refugees expelled from their homes as the state of Israel was created; and third, the 750,000 refugees pouring into Hong Kong from mainland China as a consequence of Mao Tse Tung's "Great Leap Forward." The UN was persuaded to name World Refugee Year from June 1959. In Britain, efforts made by charities such as Christian Aid and Oxfam and local churches ensured that there was good publicity, and lots of funds were raised. The main contribution of ISS UK to the call to action posed by World Refugee Year was to set up two projects: the first to help elderly refugees, and the second to assist by facilitating the adoption of Chinese orphans by British families.

In 1959, ISS UK received grants from the British World Refugee Year Committee and the Buttle Trust, and so it was able to set up a longer-term project with other refugees, many of whom were professionally trained and skilled people who, nonetheless, were unable to work in Britain and were living on meagre allowances. ISS UK gave grants for basic items that they could not afford, such as new clothing and outings for children. In the Annual Report of 1959–60, it is recorded that cases of refugees included Austrians, Bulgarians, Czechoslovakians, Estonians, Latvians, Russians, Romanians, Ukrainians, Yugoslavs, as well as lots of Poles and Hungarians.

In 1962, the government allocated £50,000 a year for the benefit of Polish ex-servicemen and women, and ISS was able to use this money to help many of the 2,000 Polish refugees it was still supporting. ISS volunteers visited many of the older people in their home and found that while many of the refugees were incredibly grateful for asylum, they still sought an independent life. After years of forced communal life, they welcomed a little privacy. ISS could help them with small allowances, for comforts and necessities, such as getting telephones installed. Eileen Lawrence and Ruth Black were two volunteers who both gave many years of help to the refugees. The programme only closed finally in 2004.

Financial stability remained a perennial concern for ISS UK, subject to external economic fluctuations and internal budgetary constraints throughout the 1970s and 1980s. Despite optimistic outlooks, financial realities often necessitated stringent measures, including staff reductions and trustee interventions to cover deficits. Fundraising, though essential, proved labour-intensive, with numerous unsuccessful grant applications during periods of economic downturns.

Case study in determination: The Libyan Family Reunion Project

The Libyan Family Reunion Project was initiated in 1996 by the Foreign and Commonwealth Office (FCO) in response to the abduction of children from Britain to Libya, leading to severed contact between parents and children. The project aimed to facilitate contact between British mothers and Libyan fathers, emphasizing the importance of maintaining relationships between noncustodial parents and children across international borders.

The absence of Libya's adherence to the Hague Convention on International Child Abduction posed legal challenges, compelling the need for diplomatic intervention. In 1997, collaborative efforts between ISS UK, the FCO, and the Higher Committee for Children (HCC) in Libya laid the groundwork for the project's implementation. Despite initial hurdles, including visa delays and logistical complexities, the first visit in September 1997 enabled fathers to reunite with their children in the UK, albeit with mixed outcomes.

The project's success hinged on ISS UK's intermediary role, facilitating communication and addressing legal and cultural sensitivities. Subsequent visits to Libya in 1998, 2000, and 2003 underscored the project's gradual progress in rebuilding familial relationships, despite persistent challenges such as language barriers and conflicting loyalties.

The resumption of diplomatic relations between the UK and Libya in 1999 facilitated direct travel, enabling greater accessibility for participants. However, the project's sustainability relied heavily on ISS UK's expertise and collaboration with the HCC, ensuring the smooth coordination of visits and resolution of outstanding issues.

Despite the project's modest scale, its significance lay in its adherence to ISS's principles of individualised support and humanitarian assistance. Efforts to expand the project to other countries, such as Cairo in 2002, reflected a broader commitment to addressing international family disputes and fostering reconciliation.

The project's enduring legacy lies in its recognition of the complex dynamics surrounding international family reunification and its role in promoting understanding and collaboration between diverse cultural contexts. While challenges persisted, the project's impact extended beyond familial reunification, fostering greater cooperation and trust between the nations and individuals involved.

Despite financial setbacks, ISS UK was determined to survive, so the organisation sought greater reliance on voluntary contributions and donations to keep services accessible to those in need. To better illustrate the impact of its work, ISS UK transitioned to Children and Families Across Borders (CFAB) on December 31, 2009. Despite initial hesitations surrounding the loss of the familiar ISS moniker, CFAB emerged with a clear identity rooted in its commitment to protecting children and uniting families across borders.

Under the leadership of Harvey McGrath, who assumed the presidency in 2009, CFAB navigated this transformative period with vigor and purpose.

The transition saw the previous ISS UK board seamlessly transition into the first board of trustees for CFAB, with Doug Lewis leading the charge. The ongoing challenge remained in balancing service provision with financial sustainability, navigating the tension between funding priorities and service demands. The transition also presented opportunities for fundraising expansion, leveraging CFAB's expertise to host impactful events and explore diverse funding streams. Meanwhile, strategic collaborations with governmental bodies and voluntary organisations bolstered CFAB's advocacy efforts and contributed to legislative discussions.

Looking back, the evolution from ISS GB's inception in 1955 to CFAB's emergence highlighted the adaptability and resilience required to navigate changing social landscapes and legal frameworks. The essence of the organisation's mission remained steadfast, grounded in the protection and welfare of children and families across borders.

Inheriting ISS UK's ethos and principles, CFAB remained committed to its nonpartisan, nonsectarian, and nonprofit mandate. Its role within the broader ISS network ensured continued collaboration and knowledge-sharing, while its contributions to social work in the UK underscored its enduring commitment to excellence.

As CFAB embarked on its journey, it embraced the enduring philosophy and principles that had guided ISS UK for decades. The organisation's leadership structure prioritised expertise in social work, fundraising, and advocacy, ensuring a holistic approach to its multifaceted mission.

Conclusion

The very founding of the ISS network is a testament to the triumph of the human spirit. The continued challenges and resultant triumphs of ISS members around the world, forged through their resilience to overcome, shines a beacon of light illuminating the path towards a brighter, more compassionate world.[38]

---

38. Special thanks to Ruth Larned, author of "International Social Service. A History 1921–1955," and Margaret Bryer, author of *An Imaginative Co-operation: The History of the International Social Service of the United Kingdom 1955–2009* (Etica Press Limited, 2015), for providing information utilised in this chapter.

Chapter 9: Expertise to Advocate

Jeannette Wöllenstein-Tripathi, Director, International Reference Centre (IRC), ISS General Secretariat

Beatriz Santaemilia del Hoyo, Child's Rights Specialist, IRC, ISS General Secretariat

Fanny Baert, COO and Director Communications, ISS General Secretariat

Advocating on behalf of the rights of persons in vulnerable situations, in particular, children and their families, has been and remains at the core of ISS action. ISS conceives and implements its advocacy work through different means, not solely through advocacy initiatives towards different entities at international, regional, and national levels, but also through its individual casework, research, or its operational capacity building and technical assistance projects. Unlike other organisations, the feature of ISS advocacy lies in the fact that it is grounded in research and practice, and seeks to address the realities of the people it serves, hereby influencing laws, policies, and most importantly, practice.

This chapter provides illustrations of ISS's advocacy work over the decades and gives an insight into ISS's crucial role in shaping key international standards in the field of children's rights and its continued evidence-based advocacy work on behalf of children. These examples focus on international activities and are in no way to be seen as exclusive.

The child's rights landscape is changing fast, requiring constant flexibility and adaptations. ISS's expertise to advocate and raise its voice with and for the most vulnerable, disadvantaged, or invisible remained steadfast throughout the decades, continues in current times, and will continue beyond its centennial celebrations.

In the early years

Since its early years, ISS has played a pioneering role in championing evidence-based advocacy and advocating for impactful change in the realm of children's rights, family protection, and migration. Through the publication and dissemination of technical and expert reports, ISS has been at the forefront of influencing legislation and policymaking globally.[39] In 1921, the London-based Standing Migration Committee of the Young Women's Christian Association (that would in 1924 become the International Migration Service and then ISS) conducted a preliminary survey on the problems faced by migrants in places including the port of Marseilles and the French-Italian border.[40] The findings of the preliminary survey were shared with the Health and Transit Sections of the League of Nations, the predecessor of the United Nations.

Later, recognising the need for a more comprehensive examination, the Standing Migration Committee entrusted Mary Hurlbutt, an American social worker and one of the founding members of ISS in 1924, with the task of conducting a thorough survey of the migration process across France, Germany, Czechoslovakia, Poland, and Switzerland. Her seminal report, "The Welfare of Migrants," was published on August 21, 1921, and submitted to the International Emigration Commission of the International Labour Organisation.

It was also in the 1920s, following its foundation in 1924, that IMS/ISS began publishing "Les Migrants," an annual publication encompassing core activities, technical insights, and a financial report. "Les Migrants" was the forerunner of today's ISS annual Global Report. The 1927 edition of "Les Migrants," for example, covered topics such as ten years of migration, field visit reports, special studies, and a detailed description of the activities of the then national ISS branches of the USA, Czechoslovakia, France, Greece, and Poland.[41]

---

39. Fanny Baert and Beatriz Santaemilia, "100 Years of Pioneer Advocacy Through Publications, Evidence-Based Research, and Action," International Social Service, February 27, 2024, https://100yearsiss.org/news/100-years-of-pioneer-advocacy.

40. Heide Fehrenbach, "Children as Casework: The Problem of Migrating and Refugee Children in the Era of World War," in Research Handbook on Child Migration, ed. Jacqueline Bhabha, Daniel Senovilla Hernandez, and Jyothi Kanics. (Edward Elgar, 2018), 23–36.

41. Larned, "International Social Service, A History, 1921–1955."

ISS Archives hold information on the participation of one of its renown figures, Suzanne Ferrière, who would become field secretary of the IMS in the mid- to late 1920s during the drafting process of the 1924 Geneva Declaration of the Rights of the Child, a crucial milestone that laid the groundwork for the evolving perception of children as rights holders, which would later be confirmed by the UN Convention on the Rights of the Child.

Between 1925 and 1926, the ISS network prepared a series of study reports directed at different institutions including the League of Nations and the International Labour Organisation (ILO) to influence international policymaking but also enact reforms in national legislation, policies, and administrative procedures with regard to migration. These reports were rich and specific as they were based on the numerous cross-border cases handled by the first ISS members. "Social Problems of Migrating Children" (1925), "Children in Transit" (1925), "Separated Families" (1926), and "The Desertion and Repatriation of Children" (1926), to name a few, were among these first reports.[42]

In the 1930s, ISS members engaged in advocacy regarding the need for a maintenance convention and for the assistance to refugees. Before the outbreak of World War II – during which most ISS branches were closed or "nationalised" – ISS led two training schools.

In the 1950s, 1960s, and 1970s

Based on its practical experience over the years to help facilitate the placement of children deprived of parental care through intercountry adoption in support of public authorities, ISS regularly pointed out the inadequacy of applicable national and international rules and their poor implementation. Consequently, ISS was "the international organisation most involved in the reflection on [intercountry] adoption as a response to the existence of children without parents, while making sure of a certain number of guarantees."[43] This advocacy was conducted by ISS towards

---

42. Larned, "International Social Service, A History, 1921–1955."

43. Yves Denéchère, "Regulating a particular form of migration at the European level: the Council of Europe and intercountry adoptions (1950–1967)," in *Peoples and Borders: Movement of Persons in Europe, to Europe, from Europe (1945–2015)*, November 2014, Padova, Italy, submitted January 7, 2015: 5, https://shs.hal.science/halshs-01101137.

newly created international and regional institutions, such as the UN as well as the Council of Europe.

Since the late 1950s, ISS took part in several meetings and expert groups on intercountry adoption, for example, the Leysin Seminar on Inter-Country Adoption in 1960. Further into the 1960s, ISS was instrumental and participated in the UN Expert Group, which for the first time identified twelve fundamental principles in intercountry adoption that laid crucial groundwork for the 1967 European Convention on the Adoption of Children as well as the later Hague Convention on Intercountry Adoption matters.

Also, in 1962, ISS prepared a special study on the problems and adjustments of migrant workers to the attention of the Council of Europe.

In the early 1980s, 1990s, and early 2000s

ISS has been and continues to be a pivotal force in shaping and implementing relevant international standards in the field of children's rights.

For instance, in 1979, ISS participated in various drafting sessions at the Hague Conference on Private International Law (HCCH) for the development of the Convention of 1980 on the Civil Aspects of International Child Abduction. Ever since, ISS members work at preventing and addressing child abduction cases and advocating for solutions in the best interests of children – as shown through a more recent advocacy example as outlined later in the chapter.

ISS's commitment towards influencing the standards applicable to respect, protect, and fulfil the human rights of children continued with full force in the 1980s. For instance, ISS was part of the NGO group that contributed to the drafting and adoption process of the 1986 Declaration on Social and Legal Principles relating to the Protection and Welfare of Children, with Special Reference to Foster Placement and Adoption Nationally and Internationally, and more importantly of the UN Convention on the Rights of the Child. ISS provided crucial input on what is known today as Article 21 of the UN Convention on the Rights of the Child.

Further, ISS has also been instrumental in the shaping of the provisions of the 1993 and 1996 Hague Conventions. Indeed, in 1990, ISS was present at the first meeting of the HCCH Special Commission on Intercountry

Adoption. What is now the wording of the second paragraph of the Preamble of the Convention – "Recalling that each State should take, as a matter of priority, appropriate measures to enable the child to remain in the care of his or her family of origin" – was notably influenced by the ISS's proposal concerning the importance of the child's birth family.

It was also during the negotiations of the 1993 Hague Convention that the idea of establishing a centre at ISS to "develop and implement international standards relating to the alternative care of children deprived of their family" started to grow. And it was in 1994, during the First Meeting of the Special Commission on the implementation of the 1993 Hague Convention, that Chantal Saclier, working at the ISS General Secretariat at that time, presented the initiative to create the International Reference Centre (IRC) for the rights of children deprived of their family to complement the work initiated with the adoption of the 1993 Hague Convention.

Today, the IRC is a well-established and renown knowledge hub and specialised research and advocacy programme at the ISS General Secretariat, based in Geneva. It is composed of multilingual child rights specialists providing services to child protection professionals in the fields of alternative care and adoption since 1993. The IRC's principal goal is to equip these professionals on the ground by developing resources and sharing promising practices. Over the past three decades, the IRC has cultivated an in-depth expertise and a wealth of experience in developing and supporting the effective implementation of international standards and providing technical guidance to professionals from various disciplines and sectors across the globe. The main focus area of the IRC is the protection of the rights of children who are either at risk of being or have been deprived of their families.

The IRC has also been instrumental in the development of the UN Guidelines for the Alternative Care of Children, welcomed formally by the General Assembly of the UN in 2009. The Guidelines were conceived from the recognition of significant gaps in implementing the UN Convention on the Rights of the Child, especially its Article 20, for millions of children worldwide without, or at risk of losing, parental care. ISS, alongside SOS International Children's Villages and UNICEF, was foundational in bringing attention to these gaps. This collaborative effort sparked a call for the international community to unite and formulate comprehensive guidelines to address these critical issues. The Guidelines emerged after five years of discussions and negotiations involving the Committee on the Rights of the Child, child-friendly governments led by Brazil, UNICEF, experts, academics, nongovernmental organisations, and, notably, young people with care experience.[44]

ISS actively participated in consultations, expert meetings, and pivotal discussions, including the Day of General Discussion in 2005. The organisation provided invaluable contributions from its General Secretariat and network, bringing a wealth of expertise and practical insights to the Committee's deliberations. Since the Guidelines' inception, ISS, together with other leading child rights organisations, has continued to play a key role in their effective implementation, notably by developing practical tools (e.g., 2012 Moving Forward Manual[45]) or several Massive Open Online Courses (MOOCs). Today, in addition to ISS network activities to promote family support as well as family-based care solutions, at the General Secretariat of ISS, there are two intrinsically related specialised and operational programmes, "A better future is possible" and the IRC. These programs continue to work towards preventing unnecessary family separations, gradually deinstitutionalising child-care systems and ensuring quality family-based care solutions.

Until today, ISS has remained steadfast in its mission to produce reports aimed at shaping legislation and providing guidance to national authorities and international and national NGOs in effectively implementing children's rights and safeguarding children and families across borders. Over the past century, ISS has produced an extensive array of publications, including annual global reports, manuals, thematic fact sheets, evaluation mission reports, editorials, and alternative reports submitted to the UN Committee on the Rights of the Child within the frame of its periodic State review process. These publications cover a broad spectrum of issues related to children's rights and child protection, such as intercountry adoption, international family mediation, children on the move, alternative care, and the search for origins, among others.

---

44. ISS/IRC Newsletter no. 269, "Special Edition, 30th Anniversary," November– December 2023: 20, https://extranet.iss-ssi.org/wp-content/uploads/2024/01/2023_269 _Newsletter_ENG.pdf.

45. Nigel Cantwell, Jennifer Davidson, Susan Elsley, Ian Milligan, and Neil Quinn, "Moving Forward: Implementing the 'Guidelines for the Alternative Care of Children.'" (Centre for Excellence for Looked After Children in Scotland, 2012), https://iss-ssi.org /storage/2023/04/Moving-Forward_English.pdf.

ISS publications are the result of comprehensive research and analyses, cross-border expertise, and fieldwork relying on various sources of literature and resources. Moreover, ISS publications stem from a collaborative effort involving ISS General Secretariat technical staff, ISS members and members ad interim, other experts, people with lived experience, and ISS partners. Today, most of these publications are available online for free, underscoring ISS's commitment to knowledge sharing and joint advocacy.

More recent examples

ISS's advocacy and standard-setting work has continued in more recent times, especially in relation to emerging fields that keep on creating barriers to the full realisation of children's rights.

It is noteworthy to highlight ISS's pioneer role in the protection of children's rights in the context of surrogacy. Early on, ISS recognised the existence of important legal and practical gaps when it comes to respecting the rights of children born through surrogacy, despite the increasing recourse to assisted reproductive technologies, including surrogacy. Additionally, the variety of domestic responses to surrogacy has contributed to the gradual development of an international commercial surrogacy market, which, of course, holds many risks for human rights abuses. It has also led to extremely complex and delicate cross-border problems for children concerned. Yet neither the Convention on the Rights of the Child nor any other international human rights instrument deal explicitly with this question, which also leaves different interpretations and approaches open.

In 2013, ISS called for an urgent international regulation of surrogacy. In 2016, ISS launched the initiative to draw up a set of principles that could be agreed on globally to guide and inform policy and legislation. In March 2021, ISS work led to the adoption of the Verona Principles for the protection of the rights of the child born through surrogacy.[46] These principles received endorsement from the majority the CRC Committee members, further underscoring ISS's leadership in standard-setting on a global scale. Over five years, consultations were held and involved experts from the UN, governments, academics, the judiciary, practitioners from multidisciplinary backgrounds representing all regions in the world, and of course, people with lived experience. The Verona Principles are a set of

---

46. International Social Service, "Principles for the Protection of the Rights of the Child Born Through Surrogacy (Verona Principles)."

eighteen interrelated principles that are all drafted from the standpoint of children's rights. So, they are mainly inspired by and grounded in the Convention on the Rights of the Child and other relevant international human rights instruments. They are based on the premise that no child should be disadvantaged or suffer harm because of the circumstances of their birth, and provide comprehensive safeguards on how to prevent violations of the human rights of children such as discrimination, statelessness, abuse, and lack of access to origins. The principles are addressed to all States, public and private entities, civil society organisations, professionals, and individuals who are, or may be, directly or indirectly involved in surrogacy.

Among the latest standard setting and advocacy work of ISS is the ongoing development of the *Ottawa Principles* since 2023. The aim is to develop principles for protecting children and parents subject to family violence across borders, also in relation to addressing international child abduction cases or relocation cases. The background of this work is that cross-border scenarios adhere to unique dynamics, necessitating specialised attention and expertise, also due to the diverse locations of family members. This set of principles will inform practitioners and policymakers on how to deal with domestic violence at the cross-border level from a very practical point of view.

Likewise, it is worth highlighting, since 2023, the joint work of several ISS members to promote international kinship care arrangements via the concept of Equity in Permanency.[47] The latter refers to principles and recommended practices to empower child protection authorities globally to promote policies that ensure that kinship care placements, also overseas, are explored for any child who can no longer be cared for by their parent, if it is in their best interests. These principles take into consideration the fact that few protection authorities have displayed the knowledge, tools, or political will to seek kinship care placements in another state, potentially compromising the child's well-being, identity, origin, language, and culture.

And finally, an area where ISS expertise and advocacy is and will continue to be specifically required is the intersection between International Human Rights Law (IHRL) and Private International Law (PriL). ISS holds this dual expertise, placing ISS in a unique position to navigate the intersection of IHRL and PriL. This is especially relevant when dealing with complex family and child protection matters with cross-border components. This

---

47. International Social Service, "Equity in Permanency."

concrete expertise makes ISS a valuable partner capable of assisting the Committee on the Rights of the Child or the HCCH, among others, in addressing the intricate legal landscape where IHRL and private international legal considerations converge, ensuring a comprehensive and well-informed approach to complex issues within the fields of child protection, alternative care, and adoption.

ISS's ongoing commitment and collaborative efforts serve as a testament to the organisation's dedication to the protection and promotion of children's rights worldwide. Whether predicted future migration trends, climate change, emergency situations, or artificial intelligence taking over many aspects of our lives, all these trends and challenges exacerbate children's and families' vulnerabilities and are lying ahead of us. But based on its agility and long-standing experience, ISS as a global network is well-equipped to continue advocating for and supporting those most in need.

Chapter 10: Energy to Continue

Part 1 by Peter van Vliet, CEO, ISS Australia

The International Social Service (ISS) has never suffered from a lack of energy. From our first female pioneer leaders in Switzerland in 1924 to the thousands of people who have passed through our organisation in the hundred years since, the energy to continue has been key.

While the group of four women who first dared to set up ISS from scratch – "the committee on the universe" – established our international lead organisation in 1924, it was not until around the middle of the twentieth century that the first seeds of the organisation began to be emerge in Australia.

For over 65,000 years, Aboriginal and Torres Strait Islanders have lived in Australia, and they form the world's oldest living culture. More recently during the last few centuries, Australia has become a magnet for migration. Migrants came first from the British Isles in the nineteenth and first part of the twentieth centuries, effectively colonising Australia, and then from continental Europe following the mass displacement of peoples resulting from the Second World War, and more recently from Asia over the last few decades. In Australia, one in two inhabitants have a direct connection with the migrant experience whether through being born overseas themselves or having one or more parents being born overseas.

Given this strong connection to migration and migrants in Australia, ISS was always going to be needed here, particularly given Australia's long distance from many of its migration source countries.

Aileen Fitzpatrick was ISS Australia's first woman pioneer, and her energy was formidable. Born in 1897 and educated in Arts and the Classics at the University of Sydney, she was a teacher that eventually gravitated towards social work. She counted Eleanor Roosevelt as a personal friend.

As General Director, Fitzpatrick helped establish an organisation called Australian Council of International Social Service in 1946, which assisted migrants and refugees fleeing postwar Europe to settle effectively in Australia. Fitzpatrick was a formidable critic of then government policies that negatively impacted migrants and refugees, and she openly criticised Australia's then-white Australia policy, which drew sanction and criticism from governments of the time and their officials.

One story illuminates the energy and passion of this female pioneer, and it was her organisation in November 1950 of the migration to Australia of sixty-one Greek and Macedonian children. These children had been separated from their parents by the Greek civil war and were then reunified with their Australian-based families who had since migrated to Australia. Reunifying children with family across borders has always been a core tenant of the work of the International Social Service.

In 1954, Aileen Fitzpatrick retired at fifty-eight years of age. She was clearly formidable and with much energy. She assisted hundreds of individuals to settle in Australia, challenged the social mores around migrants and refugees at the time, and made powerful friends and enemies. She was ISS Australia's first female pioneer, and her energy and contribution were both immense.

Our second female pioneer was Neilma Gantner, who was a founding member of today's ISS Australia, which was established in 1954 and officially incorporated in its current incarnation in Melbourne in 1961.

Gantner was the daughter of Sidney Myer, a Belarusian-born Jewish Australian who migrated to Australia at the age of twenty-one. Sidney Myer spoke little English initially but went on to establish one of Australia's most successful retail empires – the Myer retail chain – and in doing so, created the Myer dynasty. Gantner spent her younger years in both the United States and Australia, and she attended Stanford University and studied creative writing.

Neilma Gantner's contribution was simply enormous. She attended the first meeting of the newly constituted Provisional Committee of the International Social Service for Australia in November 1954 and was elected secretary.

Obtaining sufficient funding to perform our intercountry casework was a challenge for ISS Australia in the mid-twentieth century and remains a challenge to this day. Gantner used her extraordinary influence in Melbourne, Australia, to get all her circle of friends – reportedly some 400 people – to each donate £40. Her energy and enthusiasm were infectious.

Gantner held a lifelong association with the organisation and displayed the utmost generosity to ISS Australia. All of this culminated in her becoming ISS Australia's first life member in 2008. Neilma Gantner passed away in 2015.

The third female pioneer of ISS Australia was Anne Cordner, who again displayed incredible energy and made an enormous contribution. Cordner served on the Committee of Management in the 1970s before transitioning to a part-time social worker in the organisation in 1976 following the completion of her social work degree. Cordner became noted for her expertise and sensitivity in handling complex cross-border family matters.

Cordner then held the position of Director from 1979 to 1992, which appears to be one of the longest director periods in the history of ISS Australia. She combined the role of Director with direct social work at a time when the demarcation between the role of staff and board members was less strict and more fluid.

One case that Cordner recalled was that of a young migrant couple of Spanish and French origin who had a child in Australia, but who had both died tragically in a car accident shortly after. The child, who Cordner described as "a lovely boy with big, brown eyes," had no relatives in Australia and was placed in foster care. Using ISS Australia's international family tracing expertise, Cordner eventually located his family in France and found the boy's maternal grandmother in Marseilles. Finding the maternal grandmother not quite suitable due to her living arrangements with a much younger man. ISS France then located the boy's uncle in Paris, whose family was desperate to offer a permanent home to their close relative. Cordner arranged for the transfer both with the Australian government and with the boy's foster mother, who was very reluctant to let the boy go to France. The Australian government insisted on the boy being accompanied by a French-speaking guardian on the long flight to France. And of course, Anne Cordner spoke fluent French! On arrival at Charles de Gaulle airport in Paris, the boy was mobbed by fifteen relatives and the placement was at that time a success.

ISS is at its best when it champions kinship care and the importance of belonging and identity with family and kin, regardless of borders. Children will usually thrive better with kin. Anne Cordner epitomised this philosophy.

Rupert Myer, a prominent Australian businessman and philanthropist and former President of ISS Australia, described Cordner as being "the living, breathing embodiment of everything that ISS is." With a nod from one ISS female pioneer to another, Neilma Gantner described Cordner as "a women of infinite capacity." ISS Australia was left all the better from Cordner's enormous contribution.

More recently in 2022, long-serving staff member and ISS Australia Deputy CEO, Damon Martin, has produced a moving video on International Kinship Care telling the story of Joshua, who ISS Australia reunited with his family in Borneo following the breakdown of his parental relationship in Australia. Joshua was facing life in foster care in Australia, but Damon Martin and ISS Australia reunited Joshua with his family in Borneo where he has been happy ever since. This video showed the importance of international kinship care and the incredible benefits of keeping children with families wherever possible despite borders.

There have been many other important female pioneer leaders of ISS Australia in more recent times such as Diana Carrol, Marilyn Webster, and our current long-serving President Dr. Fiona McIntosh. All have strengthened ISS Australia through periods of change and renewal and maintained our laser-like focus and mission of supporting children and families across borders.

It is this energy to contribute that has steered the ISS Australia ship. More recently, Rosa Saladino and Ann Wolner set up ISS Australia's legal service in 2012, a novel development in the ISS global network that tends to be more social work-orientated. This was an extraordinary achievement. In 2018, Rebecca Chapman, ISS Australia's then managing lawyer, began a huge task to make ISS Australia a fully fledged community legal centre. In Australia, community legal centres have a specialised and respected role in providing free legal services to vulnerable people. Community legal centres are accredited bodies and require ongoing accreditation. On becoming a community legal centre, an organisation assumes a strong reputation in the legal and community sector as being an organisation that is well governed and reputable.

This work by Rosa Saladino, Ann Wolner, and Rebecca Chapman was simply incredible. The community legal centre accreditation process took three years and included securing the support of the wider community legal sector for ISS Australia's accreditation, updating all of ISS Australia's organisational policies and procedures to make the entire organisation (not just the legal component) compliant with the high standards of being an accredited centre. The status of ISS Australia as an accredited community legal centre has held ISS Australia in good stead ever since.

The work also included developing a Reconciliation Action Plan, which formalised ISS Australia's commitment to reconciliation with Aboriginal and Torres Strait Islanders, Australia's original inhabitants and the traditional owners of our lands. Indigenous people in Australia have long been subject to harmful practices such as the forced removal of children from their families, and ISS Australia was pleased to formalise our position as allies to their just cause.

While ISS Australia, like many of our partners around the globe, has traditionally provided international social work services, our accredited legal service has strengthened ISS Australia's capacity to provide legal advice to families across borders including in the international parental child abduction area, an area in which ISS Australia specialises. The legal service is now managed by another women pioneer, Jessica Raffal, who has particular expertise in family violence and the Hague Convention (1980).

One of our contemporary social work managers and long-serving staff members, Kay Hardefeldt, has produced a powerful video telling the story of a child who experienced parental child abduction, which details the significant impact this had on that child, who is now an adult. The video discusses the trauma for children in these events and why it is so important to make children, and their best interests, central to decision-making about families. Again, ISS Australia, although small in size, is valiantly supporting and promoting the best interests of children across borders.

As a result of this incredible contribution, often by women, over many years, ISS Australia is now a professional and modern service delivery organisation and a leading member of the ISS international network. ISS Australia has also developed specific expertise in international family mediation and international parental child abduction. Just this year, through the hard work of long-serving staff member Lizzie Gray, we have launched a specialised counselling service supporting people impacted by cross-border issues, including people born through donor conception or surrogacy and intercountry adoptees. ISS Australia will continue to have the energy to help make the world a better place and always support children and families across borders.[48]

Part 2 by Ursula Rölke, CEO, ISS Germany ISD

For many ISS network members, it has not always been easy to maintain their organisational viability. Over the course of time, many member organisations have got into difficulties at some point – and some of them more than once. Nevertheless, the network and its members still exist after 100 years. Why is that? Where does the energy come from to overcome all these difficulties?

The answer is manifold – but it is noticeable that the same answers apply to many members. In brief, these are: need, trust, the people and personalities, and the ISS family. Together, these elements repeatedly have generated the energy to master difficult situations, to develop new paths, and sometimes even to re-create what has been lost.

In all the changes that social work itself has undergone over the last 100 years, and the changes in cooperation across national borders, ISS has always been needed. The requirements may have changed, but the need for cross-border support has always been there. This also means that when and where ISS organisations have disappeared, a gap has emerged. And in the best circumstances, new organisations have stepped in. There are many examples to illustrate this, and what follows is only a few of them.

Italy

After many years of struggle, in 2008, ISS Italy was, unfortunately, closed down. In spite of all the support of the ISS network and the General Secretariat, it was not possible to keep this network member continuing as a going concern. However, given the ongoing need to handle cross-border social work cases involving Italy, the network did not give up. Finally, in 2012, Defence for Children (DCI) Italy began to work with ISS. This was possible only with the efforts made by several network members, actively searching for appropriate partners in Italy. It was also assisted by the ISS

---

48. This part of the chapter draws significantly from Barbara Pertzel's *A Very Personal Service: A History of International Social Service Australia Branch 1955–2005*, (Utber & Patullo Publishing, 2010) for that period.

General Secretariat as well as two network members providing training and ISS Germany acting as a Branch of Reference and channeling cases in the first phase of the cooperation with this new partner. Since that time, DCI Italy has become a full and active member of the ISS network, adding significant expertise to the network.

Canada

ISS Canada is a typical member for its will and energy to never give up, to survive, and to adapt; in showing these qualities, they have made all the difference and have indeed been reborn like a phoenix. After a breakdown of government funding in 2007, the office of ISS Canada was closed. This occurred despite support letters from all over the world. However, (not giving up) support continued to flow to Canada from the ISS General Secretariat and network members, for example, by sending open cases to Canadian Embassies and other authorities. At the same time, and given the obvious need, one staff member working from home took up handling incoming cases, which made the ongoing need for an ISS network member in Canada visible to stakeholders. This person described her motivation as, "I knew families and children needed us in Canada and that we had a great network ready to help," and she continued, "It's like each ISS member is small, but once we join forces and work together and you look at us as a network, we are big." Finally, this energy – this work done reunifying, assessing, and protecting, with each file making a difference – proved that this work and this organisation were needed. The ongoing support from the network and our local hero made the difference and generated the necessary trust in the network. The result being that new ways were found to finance the work, and ISS Canada was reestablished and is back as a strong and vital member of the network.

Germany

A major crisis was, of course, connected with World War II, but in fact, the troubles began a few years before the war commenced in 1939. In 1936, ISS Germany was excluded from the network because there was no longer any guarantee of ideological neutrality after the *Gleichschaltung*, or turning Germany into a single-party country under Hitler and the Nazi Party. This step is unique in the history of the network – but even this step testifies to the network's energy and willpower to preserve and enforce its principles.

But it also depends on people: After the expulsion, there was a great deal of contact and cooperation between network members and the German director. There was no doubt about her personal integrity, and she continued to play an important role in an informal way by maintaining contact with Poland and other neighboring countries occupied by Germany.

The need, which was even more apparent after the Second World War, was already evident at this time. And the need – with the help of the network – then gave rise to the necessary energy to develop solutions. Millions of people were stranded in Germany and its neighboring country, Austria. Thousands of children were waiting to be reunited with their families. Forced labourers and people displaced from their living space were striving to go to other countries. Many wished to return to their country of origin and others to migrate on to Australia, the US, or other countries on the American continent.

Helping to find solutions for these people required communication between specialised agencies and authorities. The IRO (International Refugee Organisation), which was primarily responsible for this, was soon looking for support, especially for social issues, and there was the existing ISS network and the confidence that ISS would be up to the task. ISS responded to this need and developed the means to take on this new, huge task. Initially an ISS delegation, consisting of the General Secretariat and members supported by German experts, set up several offices in Germany and Austria. In the 1950s, this gave rise to the new German branch office. Without the cohesion of the network on the one hand and the trust in its integrity on the other, this development would not have been possible. ISS Germany has tried to give back this support through the network by supporting other members, for example, Italy. ISS Germany is now a leading and highly regarded member of the ISS network.

There are many more examples throughout the world of ISS members struggling with adversity and surviving, or sometimes falling but often being reborn; the three examples above are, of course, not the full story. The essence is that the ISS network is very special in terms of dedicated staff making the difference. It is the people working together in ISS who generate the necessary energy to overcome crises and adapt to new situations. This is the ISS way – our energy to continue.

Chapter 11: The Next 100 Years

Jean Ayoub, ISS Secretary General and CEO

"The only constant in life is change." – Attributed to Heraclitus

Designing the ISS of the future

In the current ever-changing world, social work organisations are frequently pressed to transform themselves to be relevant in what they do. This chapter delves into strategies for the International Social Service (ISS) to maintain relevance and efficiency amidst the dynamic social challenges. Through a synthesis of existing literature and best practices, mostly written by ISS members globally, this chapter delineates key focal points for ISS encompassing embracing technology; adapting to emerging needs; strengthening global partnerships and network development; investing in capacity building and training; fostering innovation and research; advocating for policy change; integrating environmental sustainability principles; engaging youth; prioritizing trauma-informed approaches; addressing intersectionality; empowering communities; upholding ethical considerations and human rights; and ensuring financial sustainability. By adopting a multifaceted approach that incorporates these strategies, ISS can augment its effectiveness, adaptability, and significance in tackling the intricate social issues confronting individuals and families worldwide.

ISS's significance with reference to the global social service landscape is evident from the various challenges that are related to the changing needs of societies together with technological advancements. This then calls for wide-ranging exploration within social service fields in terms of organisational adaptation and innovation using best practices and case studies. It is in this regard that embracing technology emerges as one of the main channels within which ISS could concentrate its activities; this includes use of digital platforms, internet-based counselling sessions, and data analytics aimed at improving the delivery of services, communication, and collaboration.

On the organisational transformation side, ISS leaders need to undertake, examine, and compare success stories in the basic "prerequisites of success." Curiosity, creativity, courage, and the desire to change are critical, as the only constant thing in life is change, and the following suggested approaches will create the environment for change.

Adapting to emerging needs entails expanding expertise into socially connected issues like mental health and migration, trauma, and search for origins, to name a few. It is crucial to ensure ISS services remains responsive to evolving social issues. Strengthening global partnerships and networks is imperative, involving collaboration with NGOs, governments, and international organisations to address global challenges and share best practices. Investing in capacity building and training ensures ISS staff are equipped with the requisite knowledge and skills to navigate evolving social landscapes.

Fostering innovation and research within ISS cultivates a culture of experimentation and evidence-based practice, while advocating for policy change amplifies ISS's impact on a broader societal level. Integration of environmental sustainability principles underscores the interconnectedness of social and environmental issues, advocating for sustainable lifestyles and policies that prioritise social equity.

Again, in a world characterised by rapid change and evolving social challenges, social service organisations like ISS must continuously adapt to remain effective in fulfilling their mission. ISS should consider an array of strategies as a must-do, investing to enhance its relevance and efficiency in addressing the complex needs of individuals and families worldwide. Let us consider some of the strategies that will help shape the ISS organisation of the future:

Embracing technology

In an increasingly digital world, embracing technology is imperative for social service organisations like ISS to enhance service delivery, communication, and collaboration. This strategy involves leveraging digital platforms for case management, providing virtual counselling sessions, and offering digital resources for clients. Furthermore, the utilisation of data analytics can aid in identifying trends, evaluating outcomes, and improving programme effectiveness. By harnessing technology, ISS can increase its reach, efficiency, and impact in addressing social issues.

Adapting to emerging needs

ISS must stay abreast of emerging social issues and adapt its services accordingly. This includes expanding expertise in areas such as digital citizenship, online safety, and mental health support for digital natives. Additionally, ISS should address challenges posed by technology, migration, and globalisation to ensure its services remain responsive to evolving social needs. By continually adapting to emerging needs, ISS can remain relevant and effective in supporting individuals and families facing new challenges.

Global partnerships and network development

Strengthening partnerships with other NGOs, governments, academic institutions, and international organisations is essential for ISS to leverage resources, share best practices, and coordinate efforts in addressing global social challenges. Participation in global networks focused on issues like child welfare, migration, and human rights facilitates collaboration and enhances ISS's capacity to make a meaningful impact on a global scale. From this "breeding ground," ISS can train and recruit reliable members to expand its worldwide network and its global outreach.

Capacity building and training

Investing in ongoing professional development and training for staff is crucial to ensure they are equipped with the knowledge, skills, and tools needed to address evolving social issues effectively. This includes training in areas such as cultural competency, trauma-informed care, and digital literacy. By investing in capacity building and training, ISS can enhance the effectiveness and professionalism of its workforce.

Innovation and research

Fostering a culture of innovation and investing in research is essential for ISS to identify promising practices, evaluate interventions, and develop evidence-based solutions to complex social problems. This involves piloting new approaches, conducting evaluations, and sharing findings with the broader social work community. By embracing innovation and enhancing its research capabilities, ISS can continuously improve its services and adapt to changing social realities.

Advocacy and policy influence

Continuing to advocate for policies and practices that promote social justice, protect human rights, and address the needs of vulnerable populations is integral to ISS's mission. This involves engaging in policy dialogue, conducting advocacy campaigns, and collaborating with policymakers to shape legislation and policies at all levels. By advocating for policy change, ISS can address systemic barriers and create a more just and equitable society.

Environmental sustainability principles

Recognising the interconnectedness of social issues with environmental sustainability is essential for ISS to effectively address the root causes of social problems. This involves advocating for environmental policies that prioritise social equity and promoting sustainable lifestyles among clients and communities. By integrating environmental sustainability principles into its work, ISS can contribute to building a more sustainable and resilient future for all.

Youth engagement

Recognising the importance of youth engagement in social change efforts, ISS should involve young people in decision-making processes, programme design, and advocacy initiatives. Empowering youth brings new ideas, perspectives, and innovative approaches to addressing social issues. Youth often have unique insights into contemporary challenges and can offer creative solutions that resonate with their peers and the broader community. This empowers young people to become agents of change and ensures that ISS's services are responsive to the needs and perspectives of the next generation. Youth is the grantee to a lasting organisation, adapting permanently to change.

Hardship and trauma-informed approaches

Integrating hardship and trauma-informed principles into all aspects of service delivery is crucial for ISS to effectively support individuals and families who have experienced trauma. This involves creating safe and supportive environments, prioritizing the well-being and self-care of staff, and adopting practices that are sensitive to the impacts of trauma on clients.

Intersectionality

Acknowledging and addressing the intersecting and overlapping dimensions of identity, privilege, and oppression is essential for ISS to provide inclusive and equitable services. This involves incorporating an intersectional lens into its practice and recognising how factors such as race, gender, sexuality, disability, and socioeconomic status intersect to influence access to resources, opportunities, and support.

Community empowerment

Strengthening efforts to build the capacity of communities to address their own social challenges is essential for ISS to promote sustainable change. This involves supporting community-led initiatives, facilitating community organizing and advocacy, and investing in grassroots organisations working to promote social justice and well-being at the local level. ISS can bring its history of resilience, its expertise in major social issues, and its promising practices to grassroot organisation at the community level and help local communities be agents of change.

Ethical considerations and human rights

Maintaining a strong commitment to ethical practice and human rights principles is fundamental to ISS's work. This involves establishing and constantly reviewing clear ethical guidelines and protocols for staff and managers, ensuring accountability mechanisms are in place, and advocating for the rights of marginalised and vulnerable populations at all levels.

Financial sustainability

Ensuring financial sustainability is essential for ISS to continue providing essential services and support to those in need over the long term. This involves diversifying funding sources, building long-term partnerships with donors and supporters, and investing in fundraising and resource mobilisation efforts.

On the soft side of things, ISS will need to tackle the following issues that will ultimately assist the organisations and its leaders to engage and succeed transformational change.

Fostering ambition

Ambitious leaders are driven by the need to succeed, often striving for personal and organisational growth. Their success is not only a reflection of their individual achievements but also of their ability to inspire and lead others towards shared goals. Ambitious leaders see success to realise their vision, overcome challenges, and make a lasting impact on their organisation and beyond. They set high standards for themselves and their teams, pushing boundaries and exploring new opportunities for innovation and advancement.

For ambitious leaders, success is not just a destination but an ongoing journey of continuous improvement and excellence. It fuels their passion, determination, and resilience in the face of obstacles, driving them to overcome adversity and achieve their aspirations. Ultimately, the success of ambitious leaders is measured not only by tangible outcomes but also by the legacy they leave behind and the positive change they bring to their organisation and the world. ISS was founded on such ambition, vision, and the courage to dare. Our legacy as current leaders is to perpetuate that message across future generations.

Celebrating success

Celebrating successes serves multiple purposes within an organisation. It boosts morale by acknowledging the hard work and dedication of team members, creating a positive work environment. Additionally, it reinforces the organisation's purpose and vision, reminding everyone of their collective goals and maintaining focus on the mission. Moreover, it builds team cohesion by fostering camaraderie and trust among senior management and staff, while also motivating performance by providing positive reinforcement for desired behaviours and outcomes.

Furthermore, celebrating success drives engagement by making employees feel valued and appreciated, leading to higher levels of commitment. Last, when senior management actively participates in celebrating success, it sets a powerful example for the rest of the organisation, reinforcing the importance of recognising and rewarding excellence at all levels.

Cultivating empathy

Empathy is vital during organisational change as it involves understanding and sharing others' feelings, perspectives, and experiences. Empathetic leaders listen to employees' concerns, fears, and uncertainties about change, building trust by showing genuine care and attention to their well-being. They encourage open communication, allowing employees to express themselves and providing valuable insights into how changes are perceived.

Empathy helps address resistance to change with understanding, acknowledging concerns, and finding solutions that balance organisational goals with employee needs. It fosters inclusivity by recognising and respecting diverse perspectives, creating a culture where everyone feels valued and included. Overall, empathy enables leaders to navigate change successfully by building trust, fostering communication, addressing resistance, promoting inclusivity, and ultimately leading to more successful change initiatives.

Building resilience

Resilience is the ability to bounce back from setbacks, adapt to change, and thrive in the face of adversity. In the context of organisational change, resilience is crucial for individuals, teams, and the organisation. Overall, resilience is essential for individuals, teams, and organisations to thrive amid change. By cultivating adaptability, problem-solving skills, emotional regulation, flexibility, support networks, learning orientation, and a sense of purpose, organisations can build resilience and successfully navigate the challenges and opportunities that come with change.

Advocating for solidarity

Solidarity is crucial in a network like ISS because it promotes collaboration, mutual support, and collective action towards common goals. Solidarity strengthens relationships among member organisations, enhancing effectiveness by leveraging diverse expertise and resources. Solidarity simplifies our differences and helps us concentrate on the most important goals, ensuring support for families in children, advocating for their rights, and building trust and credibility within and outside the network. Solidarity also fosters resilience during crises, promoting learning and innovation. Ultimately, solidarity enables ISS member organisations to achieve greater impact and positively impact the lives of those they serve.

Flexibility and agility

Maintaining flexibility and agility are vital for organisations like ISS to succeed in addressing complex social issues. ISS can foster flexibility by cultivating adaptive leadership, developing responsive programmes, and leveraging strategic partnerships. Embracing technology, cross-training staff, and nurturing a learning culture also enhance agility. By streamlining decision-making processes, planning for resilience, and staying attuned to emerging needs, ISS can adapt swiftly to changing circumstances and continue to effectively support vulnerable populations worldwide.

In a nutshell, social work organisations like our ISS must adapt the ways they collaborate and deliver work because the world around us is constantly changing. People's needs, society's challenges, and the tools available to help them are always evolving. By staying flexible and open to new ways of working together, ISS can better meet the needs of the communities its members serve. Collaboration allows different organisations and individuals to bring their unique strengths and perspectives to the table, creating more effective solutions to complex problems.

Additionally, adapting how work is delivered ensures that services remain relevant and accessible in a rapidly changing world, ultimately helping more people and making a positive impact on society.

In conclusion, by integrating these soft skills and strategic approaches into its operations, ISS can bolster its effectiveness, adaptability, and significance in tackling the dynamic social issues impacting individuals and families globally. As ISS navigates a swiftly evolving world, it must uphold a steadfast dedication to innovation, collaboration, and social justice to fulfill its mission and foster positive transformations in communities worldwide. To achieve this, ISS must invest in cultivating or identifying and nurturing multiskilled leaders who not only excel in core competencies but also demonstrate proficiency in negotiation, communication, and innovation. These leaders should possess ambition and creativity, driving ISS's growth and impact in addressing the diverse needs of vulnerable children and families.

ISS network has already taken significant steps towards embracing change and implementing necessary adaptations to meet the evolving needs of children, families, and communities it serves. For instance, ISS has been actively integrating technology into its operations to enhance service delivery and communication. This includes the use of digital platforms for case management, offering virtual counselling sessions, and utilizing data analytics to improve programme effectiveness.

Furthermore, ISS has been consolidating its expertise to better address emerging social issues such as migration challenges for children moving alone, family violence, international child abduction, and the search for origins in matters of adoption, to name just a few of today's challenges! By broadening its scope of services, ISS ensures that it remains responsive to the changing needs of individuals and families worldwide.

Additionally, ISS has been strengthening its global partnerships and networks, collaborating with NGOs, governments, and international organisations to address global social challenges and share best practices. This collaboration not only leverages resources but also fosters learning and innovation, ultimately enhancing ISS's capacity to make a meaningful impact on a global scale.

ISS is providing training and development opportunities for its staff to ensure they have the right skills to adapt to changing social needs. This investment in professional growth helps create a culture of excellence and professionalism within the organisation.

Overall, ISS's proactive approach to change and innovation demonstrates its commitment to remaining relevant, adaptable, and impactful in addressing the complex needs of individuals and families locally and globally. Through these efforts, ISS continues to uphold its mission of promoting social justice and positive transformations in communities around the world.

Looking ahead to the future of ISS, we must stay flexible and open to change. By using new technology, adapting to what people need, and working closely with others worldwide, ISS can keep helping families and individuals facing tough times. We also need to make sure our staff have the right skills and keep finding better ways to do things. This includes being creative, speaking up for what is right, and being mindful of how our actions affect the environment. We should involve young people, be sensitive to people's past traumas, and remember everyone's different backgrounds and needs. By working together, staying adaptable, and caring for our planet and one another, ISS can keep making a positive difference in people's lives around the world.

"The greatest danger in times of turbulence is not the turbulence itself, but to act with yesterday's logic."

— Peter Drucker

About International Social Service

International Social Service (ISS), founded in Geneva in 1924, is a non-governmental, nonsectarian, nonprofit, and independent membership organisation. ISS is a worldwide network of professional organisations working together to protect, defend, and support children, families, and individuals separated as a consequence of cross-border migration. ISS aims to ensure that respect for human rights is accorded to ail individuals, particularly children.

Contact

info@iss-ssi.org

Connect with us

Website: https://iss-ssi.org

LinkedIn: https://www.linkedin.com/company/international-social-service

Facebook: https://www.facebook.com/ISSGeneralSecretariat

Instagram: https://www.instagram.com/issgeneralsecretariat

About

PEN & PUBLISH

Pen & Publish started as a small press dedicated to publishing work by or for schools and nonprofits in 2005, and thoroughly enjoy publishing several schools' annual student anthologies. In addition to adding traditional imprints, we now also offer custom publishing services to authors, small presses, and organizations.

Our Imprints

Open Books Press publishes nonfiction for adults and fiction for all ages, and Transformation Media Books publishes work in the body, mind, and spirit genres. Brick Mantel Books, added in 2015, is dedicated to publishing quality literary fiction and poetry.

Contact

We are always interested in hearing your feedback. We can also coordinate requests for in-person or virtual author appearances, book club or bulk purchases, and bookstore or library orders. Email us at info@penandpublish.com.

Connect with us

Website: https://penandpublish.com

Monthly Newsletter: http://eepurl.com/iY_VOI

Facebook: https://www.facebook.com/PenandPublishLLC

Instagram: https://www.instagram.com/penandpublishllc

Youtube: https://www.youtube.com/@penandpublish

www.ingramcontent.com/pod-product-compliance
Lightning Source LLC
Chambersburg PA
CBHW070127030426
42335CB00016B/2287